# RAISING CHICKENS

## The Essential Guide

Taliah
Drayak

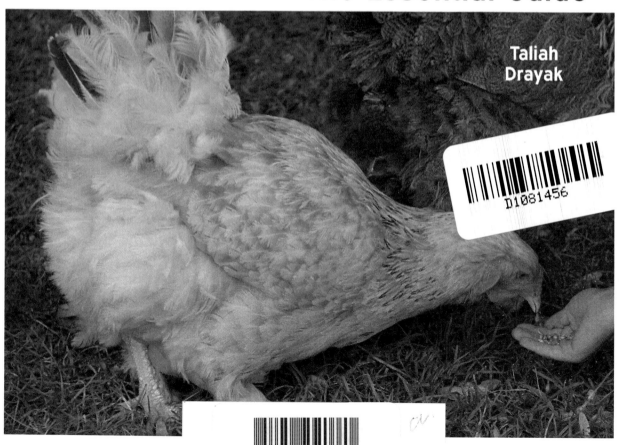

*Raising Chickens: The Essential Guide* is also available in accessible formats for people with any degree of visual impairment. The large print edition and e-book (with accessibility features enabled) are available from Need2Know. Please let us know if there are any special features you require and we will do our best to accommodate your needs.

First published in Great Britain in 2013 by
Need2Know
Remus House
Coltsfoot Drive
Peterborough
PE2 9BF
Telephone 01733 898103
Fax 01733 313524
www.need2knowbooks.co.uk

# Contents

# Introduction

Are you able to spare five minutes each morning and evening? Do you have an extra half hour at the weekends? Do you enjoy animals and want to treat them with kindness and empathy? If you want a pet that won't need walking in the rain, then perhaps a chicken is the right choice for you.

If you have previously cared for a pet rabbit you may already have the run and facilities necessary to allow your chickens room to exercise. Although chickens need housing with perches and nesting boxes, a rabbit hutch and run can be easily converted into poultry accommodation.

Chickens are easy to keep in even small gardens. They need very little equipment aside from a safe dry home. A noisy cockerel need not be a cause for concern as hens will lay quite well without one. With a little care, chickens will provide the whole family with an undemanding and generous pet. Chickens are full of character and will provide more than just breakfast as they entertain and delight you with their play.

As the price of food continues to rise, and people look for ways to take part in producing their own food, the number of chickens living in towns and cities is rising. Eggs are a nutritious food and staple ingredient. From home-made beauty products to poached eggs on toast, the versatility of eggs is hard to beat. For those who take pride in their gardens, chickens can be an excellent asset as they eat common pests and produce high-quality natural fertiliser.

Our domestic chickens' forefather began in the jungles of South Asia somewhere around 5000 BC. It was the Cochin chickens from China, that were gifted to Queen Victoria and gave rise to the trend of British chicken keeping. Having traded roosting in trees for hand sanded perches, these curious and social creatures are now becoming popular in urban homes.

This easy-to-read book is written for those keeping chickens, both beginner and novice. If you are starting out with a small flock of chickens for the first time, then this book is written with you in mind. It contains an honest and forthright overview of everything that you need to know about caring for chickens on a day-to-day basis. From mixing your own feed to caring for your

'With a little care, chickens will provide the whole family with an undemanding and generous pet.'

chickens should they become ill, this book is filled with information gleaned from experience. We will look at hatching and rearing chicks and how to care for the broody hen. The book will help you to prepare for your chickens ahead of their arrival to ensure everyone has a safe and stress-free first day at home. There is a chapter dedicated to choosing a breed to suit your individual needs, and one to help when you run out of ideas about what to do with all those fresh eggs. You can find guidance on all aspects of animal welfare and Defra in clear and easy to understand language in the last chapter.

## Disclaimer

'As the price of food continues to rise, and people look for ways to take part in producing their own food, the number of chickens living in towns and cities is rising.'

This book is written as a general guide to chicken care. It is not intended to replace professional veterinary advice. If you suspect your chicken is ill it is important to contact your local veterinarian to obtain a quick and accurate diagnosis. All the information given in this book was correct at the time of going to press. Defra regulations and local guidelines are subject to change and as such it is important to contact your local council ahead of bringing home any livestock animal.

# Chapter One

# Why Keep Chickens?

## Not just for farms

Raising chickens is proving to be a popular pastime, and it is easy to see why. According to the British Hen Welfare Trust there has been an 80 percent growth in the rehoming of chickens over the last three years. Today, over 700,000 people are keeping domestic chickens. Whether for egg production, companionship, conservation, exhibiting, or concerns about animal welfare, people are allowing poultry into their hearts and home gardens.

The domestication of chickens began over 4,000 years ago. Records in Britain date back centuries, though it was the Victorians that began documenting their efforts in achieving and improving breed standards. Today, there are hundreds of breeds available for purchase, most of which are readily available. With long tails, bold combs and dazzling plumage in a wide variety of colours and markings, you could, should you so wish, choose to coordinate them with your household decor! More information on breeds and breed characteristics will be looked at in detail in chapter 2.

Chickens are omnivores and will eat almost any food you give them. This can help you reduce both your food waste and your carbon footprint. Proper feeding and nutrition will be discussed fully in chapter 3.

Chickens require only a few minutes each day. Add a half hour a week to clean their house and they are not much more trouble than a pet hamster. They enjoy having their feathers stroked like a cat, but never request a dog's wet early morning walk. Their genial clucking and quirky characters will soon have you smitten.

'Whether for egg production, companionship, conservation, exhibiting, or concerns about animal welfare, people are allowing poultry into their hearts and home gardens.'

# Fresh eggs

According to the British Egg Information Service, there are more than 32 million eggs eaten each day in the UK. Eggs are a dietary staple that we spend over 700 million pounds per year purchasing.

## Why eat eggs?

Eggs play an important role in our diet because:

- Eggs are a great source of high-quality protein.
- They provide 13 essential nutrients.
- Eggs are one of the few foods which contain vitamin D. Vitamin D promotes calcium absorption and plays an important role in bone growth, neuromuscular and immune function.
- They are a low-calorie food containing just 80 calories per egg.
- Eggs are no longer considered a risk to cholesterol levels. Research cited from the British Heart foundation suggests eating eggs may lower blood pressure.

'There are more than 32 million eggs eaten each day in the UK. Eggs are a dietary staple that we spend over 700 million pounds per year purchasing.'

There's a lot of dispute over the nutritional differences between commercial and home-grown eggs. These days, supermarket eggs are of high quality, and yet, every chicken keeper will tell you how much better their eggs taste. The indisputable fact is that industrial egg farms are businesses at the mercy of making a profit. Consumers assume that free-ranging hens pass their days scratching worms out of the earth and running about in the sunshine. Unfortunately, profit margins are so narrow that many farmers are unable to provide the level of quality care to which both they, and their chickens, might aspire. Whether the difference is genuine or not, eggs produced by your beloved hen will be appreciated and enjoyed.

Poaching a freshly collected egg from a hen you have reared, is deeply satisfying. To know your food has been grown in a healthy way, and to take an active role in its production, is to reclaim a part of our heritage which has been pushed aside by our hectic modern life. The uses for eggs are plentiful. How to use and store eggs, will be discussed more fully in chapter 9.

Certain breeds lay more frequently than others. Leghorns, of good breeding, may lay 360 eggs a year whereas Indian game hens may produce as few as 60. It would be misleading to suggest that raising a small flock of chickens will have a significant financial benefit. The cost of keeping a chicken is very low. However, as with any pet, it is easy to find new ways to indulge them. By keeping to a careful budget, however, chickens can be a rewarding pet, and provide modest savings.

## Slug patrol

Gardeners lament year after year as their gardens are blighted by ants, aphids, greenfly, beetles, spider mites, slugs and more. Gardeners who raise chickens no longer have to worry about these pests. There are very few insects that a chicken will not happily dine on.

If you have a vegetable garden, chickens can be a great asset at the start and close of your growing season. Hens will take great pleasure in breaking up your freshly turned over soil. They will clear the ground of all pests and most weeds, and produce excellent fertiliser. The plant 'chickweed' was named for its popularity with chickens. And should you have a bumper vegetable crop, chickens will ensure that none of your surplus will go to waste.

Of course, when your vegetables are growing beautifully, chickens will enjoy every beak full of your strawberries and lettuces. Depending on the size of your garden it will be up to you as to whether you would prefer to fence off the garden or to build a run. Securing your garden to protect both chickens and plants will be looked at in more detail in chapter 4. There are a number of plants which are toxic to poultry, and these will be discussed in detail in chapter 7.

'By keeping to a careful budget chickens can be a rewarding pet, and provide modest savings.'

## An addictive hobby

It all starts with a trio of hens. They will charm you with their amiable chatter, soft plumage and delicious eggs. Before you know it, you will find yourself dreaming of adding new chickens of varying characteristics to the flock. Thoughts of blue eggs at breakfast might lead you to add an Araucana. The fantasy of having a pair of bearded birds peeking out amongst your daffodils may bring you to add a couple of Faverolles. In the spring it is easy to imagine small fluffy chicks peeping out from beneath a protective wing. Silkies are excellent mothers who will hatch and rear up to 26 chicks at a time.

Those who keep chickens become very proud of their birds. At some point, you may decide you'd like to show your chickens. There are poultry shows, agricultural fairs, and exhibitions in every county. Even if you are not keen on showing your birds, attending events such as these are a great opportunity to meet people in your local community and learn more about chickens. If you are planning on breeding your chickens, taking time to become familiar with breed standards will help to maintain generations of hard work and improve the lines that are currently in circulation.

'If you are planning on breeding your chickens, taking time to become familiar with breed standards will help to maintain generations of hard work and improve the lines that are currently in circulation.'

# Great with children

Caring for a pet is a right of passage, and hens are an excellent choice. They are easy to care for, and resilient to gentle cuddling. Hens are specifically mentioned, as cockerels can be less friendly. If you are not interested in breeding, a cockerel is not necessary for egg laying.

## Why choose chickens?

- They will offer children the chance to practise discipline, responsibility and routine. All animals must be cared for morning and night. Their house needs regular cleaning, and they need access to food and water. Chickens have simple needs and most children are able to help with some aspect of their care.

- The experience of holding an egg still warm from being laid, will nurture the child's sense of pride in their work and teach an understanding of where food comes from.

- The best way to care for any animal is to spend time getting to know them. Children can learn about individual personalities and how to interact with them.

- Hens enjoy being loved and will offer affection in return. Children enjoy giving love and receiving affection.

- There is the potential to teach children the basics of budgeting and business. Older children are quick to pick up on how much things cost. Helping them to keep a record of how much the chickens' upkeep costs in relation to the number of eggs produced can teach them life skills.

## How to interact with chickens

- Offer treats by hand to encourage the chickens to associate you as their food source.

- Chickens can become excited by the colour red. By choosing trousers or leggings which are not red or red spotted, the chickens will not have any inclination to peck at yours or a child's legs.

- Always wash your hands after handling birds or their bedding. It is very unlikely that any disease or illness will be passed on, but basic hygiene is important when handling any animal.

- Chickens enjoy music. Try singing to them and they will soon start to sing along with you too.

- When picking up a chicken hold it firmly by the body. Keep both wings tucked in and hug the chicken close to your chest.

## What are the difficulties in keeping chickens?

Chickens are not litter trainable like cats and dogs. A chicken will leave droppings almost anywhere. Families with young toddlers might prefer to keep their chickens in a run. Footballs are easy collectors of droppings and it is prudent not to roll them over grass the chickens are kept on.

Chickens can be overcome by extreme stress. If a child or dog chases a hen it could have a heart attack. Many chickens will go off laying during periods of stress. As with any animal, it is important to encourage children to be aware of the animal's vulnerabilities. Animal welfare will be looked at in more detail in chapter 10.

'Chickens can be overcome by extreme stress. As with any animal, it is important to encourage children to be aware of the animal's vulnerabilities.'

Cockerels have the potential to be aggressive. They are territorial and loud. Though certain breeds are more exuberant with their crowing than others, many will crow throughout the day. If you wish to keep a cock, and you have close neighbours it may be wise to check with them first.

## What about bird flu?

Many people worry about disease and illness being spread to humans by chickens. Illnesses, such as avian influenza, are not easily passed from birds to humans. Most transferable illnesses come from wild birds. Sometimes a wild bird may infect a domestic bird, but it is important to emphasise the risk is very small. If you purchase chickens from a reputable breeder they will almost certainly be vaccinated against the big three: Marek's disease, Newcastle disease and infectious bronchitis. Diseases and vaccines will be discussed at more length in chapter 6. As long as you wash your hands every time you handle your chickens or their bedding, they pose no greater health risk than any other common pet.

'Chickens can live for more than a decade and tend to become more docile as the years pass.'

## Personality to spare

Bringing chickens into your home is to welcome into your life an abundance of attitude that will forever amuse you. As inquisitive and friendly as they are naughty and bossy, chickens are not wall flowers.

Given a cob of corn, hens will play games of keep away and rugby that may distract and delight you, making it difficult to find the time to watch the real thing! They take a keen interest in their humans. If you hang your washing out at the same time each morning they will learn your habits and will be there waiting for your company. Chickens can live for more than a decade and tend to become more docile as the years pass.

They have complex social structures and are adept communicators. Each chicken has a very distinct personality and will adapt to the place it maintains in the pecking order. One chicken may be the bird that calls the flock into their house at night. Should a large bird fly over the coop, the flock guard will ensure everyone is informed. A rhythmic bock, bock, bock will alert you to a proud hen seeking praise after having laid an egg. You will quickly come to understand their clucks. The low crow they call out to you and you alone, will show they have identified you as their friend and caregiver.

Chickens live in a strictly enforced social order. There will be an alpha hen and she will not fraternise with those she deems less worthy. You can try to encourage equality, but it will be in vain. Do not lose sleep over their family dynamics, they prefer these relationships, and so long as they are not overcrowded and underfed, they will live in relative peace.

# Summing Up

- Chickens are an undemanding pet that enjoy human companionship.

- Depending on the breed, you can anticipate anywhere from 60-360 eggs per hen per year during their peak laying years.

- Eggs are a nutritious part of our diet.

- Chickens are a beautiful addition to any garden. They will turn garden beds over and keep the pest population down. While they keep the grass trimmed and the weeds pulled, you can sit and enjoy their humorous antics.

- Raising chickens can be an engaging hobby. By taking your birds to shows you can meet other people with similar interests and learn more about the breed you are keeping.

- Hens can make great children's pets. They will teach children responsibility, and about where their food comes from. Easy to tame, and easy to love, chickens encourage children to empathise.

- Cockerels are noisy. If you do not plan on breeding then consider purchasing just hens.

- There are no two chickens exactly alike. Each is as much an individual as any person. They have complex social orders within their flock and will, with a little nurturing, put you at the top of their pecking order. Chickens bond quickly to their owners and enjoying being with them.

# Chapter Two

# Choosing a Breed

There are hundreds of breeds and as such this chapter will mention the ones which are both widely available, and have proven popular. Do your research and don't hesitate to ask questions before making a decision. What works for one person may not be the best choice for another. A large garden may accommodate a diverse flock of large fowl, while a small garden may be best suited to keeping bantams. Chickens and their eggs come in a wide range of colours. If you have a preference for white, brown, blue, green, pink or speckled eggs, you will have no trouble narrowing your selection. Nonetheless, there will still be enough selection to make it difficult to select just one. Each breed has been bred for a purpose. Their unique temperaments, laying abilities, and overall hardiness should be considered when assessing if they will suit your lifestyle.

It is recommended by the Poultry Club of Great Britain that chicken keepers keep pure breeds in order to maintain and improve breed standards. By choosing a pure breed you can better anticipate the needs of your flock and how suitable they are to your needs. All reference to egg colour and annual laying abilities has been referenced from the Poultry Club of Great Britain online *A guide to pure breed chicken expected laying capabilites* (see the reference list at the end of the book). For a full and comprehensive guide to chicken breeds, go to www.omlet.co.uk and click on 'chicken breeds'. Here you will find many more breeds that could not be squeezed into a single book chapter.

## Light breeds

Light breeds are birds that have primarily originated from the Mediterranean. They tend to be great layers with soft fluffy plumage. Cocks will average 2.7-3.2kg. Hens will average 2.3-2.7kg. Temperament wise, light breeds will

'It is recommended by the Poultry Club of Great Britain that chicken keepers keep pure breeds in order to maintain and improve breed standards. By choosing a pure breed you can better anticipate the needs of your flock and how suitable they are to your needs.'

tend towards being of a nervous disposition. Their small size makes them more prone to predators, and they are more flighty. However, they tend to consume less feed in relation to the number of eggs they produce than many heavier breeds.

## Araucana

Originating from Chile, this breed is favoured for its consistent laying of blue eggs. They are hardy birds, which tolerate cold weather well, and require minimum maintenance. Araucanas are alert and friendly birds who will lay 150 eggs per year. They come in colours ranging from lavender to black and have prominent feathering around their head, muffs, tufts, beard and ears.

## Friesian

A very old Dutch breed, from the Friesian islands, the Friesian is a small robust bird. They are sociable and inquisitive. Friesians are notable for being modest eaters and good layers. A hen will lay on average 230 eggs per year. Their standard colours are gold, silver and chamois penciled.

## Leghorn

An Italian breed which has been bred in Britain since the 1800s. Leghorns are economical eaters and prolific layers. The average hen can lay in excess of 320 eggs per year. They are shy birds who prefer to keep on the go. Their plumage ranges in colour from black, blue, brown, buff, cuckoo, golden, mottled, partridge, pyle and white.

## Scots Grey

Dating back to the 16th century, Scots Grey is an old breed that may have been refined from wild birds in Scotland. They are hardy and quick maturing. Quick-winged, they will roost in a tree if they have the opportunity. Their long legs and barred markings make a very distinguished bird. A Scots Grey hen will lay about 200 tinted eggs a year. They are quite cold hardy and under the right conditions can lay through the winter.

## Silkie

Myth has it that Silkies were originally sold as a cross between a rabbit and a chicken. They sound and look rather like the original Easter bunny. Silkies are covered in fine fluffy feathers. They have a circular comb, described as a mulberry comb, and a small ragged tail. Silkies are excellent mothers. Their tendency towards broodiness is a breed characteristic. They are often kept to rear eggs from other breeds and do so with great success. Silkies are not prolific layers and will lay up to 100 small tinted eggs in a good year.

## Vorwerk

Developed by Oskar Vorwerk in Hamburg, Vorwerks will lay up to 170 cream-coloured eggs a year. They are hardy and great foragers. Vorwerks are bright and enjoy flying which may not be suitable for all gardens. They have striking plumage with the soft buff chest feathers being complimented by the molasses coloured neck and tail feathers. Originally developed to be economical eaters they are not as greedy as some of their contemporaries.

# Heavy breeds

Heavy breeds are good layers and tend to be dual purpose. They tend to be quiet and relaxed. They eat more than a light breed chicken and may lay fewer eggs. Many heavy breeds are renowned for going broody and will make great mothers. Heavy breeds have often been bred more for their table qualities than for their egg production, and as such may require specific care to avoid quickly putting on excess weight.

## Cream Legbars

A very rare and attractive blue egg layer. Legbars are making a come back in popularity after having almost become extinct. The chicks are autosexing. The dark chicks are female and the light chicks are male. The breed has been accused of being flighty in character and very active. They will lay between 150-180 eggs a year during their best years.

## Maran

Developed in France in the 1800s, they became popular for their dark brown eggs. They are lazy birds and will put on fat quickly. Hardy and disease resistant, Marans will lay up to 200 eggs per year. Marans are great with young children and are known for being keen lap birds.

'The Buff Orpington is currently one of the most popular British breeds, as it was the breed kept by Her Majesty the Queen Mother.'

## Orpington

This breed of utility chicken comes from Orpington in England. It is thought that the first Black Orpington was bred in 1886 by William Cook. The Buff Orpington is currently one of the most popular British breeds, as it was the breed kept by Her Majesty the Queen Mother. Orpingtons are very large and fluffy. Their plumage comes in over a dozen rich colours and they look like the hens you see embroidered on a tea cozy. The only downside to their downy appearance is that they must be kept out of the rain as their feathers are not water resistant. Orpington records show that they were capable of laying up to 340 eggs a year. However, as breeding has selected show quality appearances over laying, the average modern Orpington will produce up to 200 eggs a year.

## Rhode Island Red

From the US state of Rhode Island, the Rhode Island Red is the very successful offspring of a large variety of other breeds. Known for its superb egg production, they are known the world over. They have glossy red feathers and lay over 300 brown eggs a year. While they are a relatively quiet breed, they are very alert and active. The cockerels of this breed have a slightly higher than normal tendency towards aggression.

## Sussex

The Sussex breed originated in Sussex, England, and is thought to be possibly the oldest pure breed still in use. Sussex chickens can be found in a variety of colours with the white Sussex being very popular. They are an alert utility breed that are happy to free range. Sussex hens have soft gentle voices and quickly bond with their keepers. A graceful and docile chicken who love to forage. The dedication to breed standard has kept both their exceptional laying and table qualities. Sussex hens will produce up to 260 large light brown eggs a year.

## Welsummer

Welsummers were first bred in Holland along the river Ysel. They are active chickens who stand upright and hold their heads high. They are good layers and produce rich dark brown, almost deep red, eggs. The Welsummer is best known for its cockerel who became famous on the Kellogg's Cornflakes cereal box. They are friendly and intelligent chickens who will lay up to 200 eggs a year.

## Wyandotte

Wyandottes have beautifully laced feathers which makes them a very attractive chicken. They are calm birds which are well suited to domestic life. They lay up to 200 pale brown eggs in their first year of laying and are devoted mothers. Like many fluffy feathered breeds, they are prone to an accumulation of faeces around their vent and will need care and attention to avoid the area becoming obstructed.

# Hybrids

In the 1950s the commercial egg industry began breeding hybrids from just a few of the most productive pure breed lines to improve production in the battery cage farm. This has bred many hybrid breeds of hardy, and heavy egg laying chickens. Hybrid chickens tend to be far more uniform in colour and size. Hybrid chickens lay heavily in their first two years of life and tend not to have the length of life span that a pure breed may enjoy. They do tend to be quite docile birds whom will quickly adapt to being held and stroked.

## Black Rock

A cross between a Rhode Island Red and a Barred Plymouth Rock, the Black Rock is a cold hardy and productive layer. They are primarily black with brown and bronze colouring around their necks and a small single comb. They are thought to be highly disease resistant and make good use of free ranging. They lay up to 280 large brown eggs a year.

## Bluebell

A rather large hybrid chicken, Bluebells have long legs and beaks. They are productive layers and will produce up to 260 large brown eggs a year. A genuine Bluebell is a cross between a Maran and a Rhode Island Red and will often have a parma violet hue to their feathers. They are docile and friendly.

## Hyline

Hyline chickens are a commercial cross breed that has been very specifically produced for egg production. They are said to produce around 330 good sized white eggs a year. Appearance wise they are an ordinary-looking brown hen and require very little feed to produce an abundance of quality eggs.

## ISA Browns

These are a close relation to the Hyline. They are a commercial cross breed between a Rhode Island Red and a Rhode Island White. The ISA Browns are bred with battery farms in mind. Most ex-battery rescue hens are ISA Browns. They are medium sized and prolific layers. They are great converters of feed and will produce over 300 eggs a year.

## Speckledies

These hens are relatively new. They were first bred in 1992 in the UK. They were bred with the intention of finding a way to produce organic free-range eggs on a commercial basis. Speckledies are a Rhode Island Red and Maran cross and will lay up to 260 eggs a year. They have a thick insulating feather coverage which allows them to free range comfortably in cooler climates and are not well suited to small runs. Speckledies are gentle-tempered and growing in popularity among small commercial flock keepers.

## White Star

White Stars are a Dutch leghorn hybrid. They are a small pristine white chickens with a large floppy comb. They lay up to 320 medium-sized pure white eggs a year. White Stars tend to have a nervous disposition and are not the best choice for a child's first pet. Nonetheless, they get along well with other chickens regardless of size difference or flock numbers.

# Bantams

Bantams are breeds of small chickens which are well suited to smaller gardens. However, they lay less often and when they do their eggs are smaller. Several heavy breeds of chicken have a smaller 'bantam' counterpart. These chickens are one third to one quarter of the size of their larger breed equivalents. True bantams do not have a corresponding heavy breed equivalent.

## Pekin

Pekins are an endearing little bird that stand just 20-30 centimetres tall. They have feathers which grow down their legs and cover their feet. As such, care must be taken to ensure they kept clean and dry. They are great foragers and are very docile. Pekins are primarily kept as exhibition stock and will lay up to 160 small white eggs a year.

### Barbu d'Uccle

These chickens came to the UK in 1911 from a small town outside Brussels. Barbu d'Uccle is small bearded chicken with feathers growing down its legs and feet. They have a small single comb and tiny wattle. They are friendly chickens who are known for being good mothers. Barbu d'Uccles will lay up to 150 small pale eggs a year.

### Rosecomb

These chickens are proud and graceful. They have short beaks, big bold eyes, a large rose comb, and commanding white earlobes. Rosecombs are primarily exhibition stock and are not known for their mothering abilities. They will lay up to 50 tiny cream eggs a year. They like to fly and are not naturally docile.

### Sebright

The Sebright is a British bantam named after Sir John Sebright who first bred them. They are an adventurous and hardy breed of chicken, who will roost in a tree if allowed the opportunity. Sebrights are commonly kept for their ornamental value but not for their egg laying. On average a Sebright will produce up to 50 tiny white eggs.

## Ex-battery

If you want to care for ex-battery hens, then contacting the British Hen Welfare Trust is essential. Go to www.bhwt.org.uk and they will provide you with all the information needed to find a rehoming hub near you. Ex-battery hens are almost always hybrids. They will be around 70 weeks old and will have spent their life in a cramped indoor environment. They may be missing feathers, have their beak cut, and will have weakened legs. Despite their poor initial appearance you can rest assured they will be fully vaccinated and free from disease. Ex-battery hens will make your heart swell with pride as you offer a bird a new lease on life. They bloom through gentle care and will continue to lay at a diminished rate for one to three years.

'Ex-battery hens will make your heart swell with pride as you offer a bird a new lease on life. They bloom through gentle care and will continue to lay at a diminished rate for one to three years.'

# Game breeds

Game birds have short tightly feathered bodies. Their slender silhouette descends from ancient fighting cocks. Their temperament is generally quite calm amongst hens, though keeping multiple cocks would be unsuitable. Game hens are acceptable layers and are very protective mothers. Game breeds are good foragers and will free range.

## American

The American game hen is considered by those who keep them to be the very finest mother a chick could ask for. They are frequently broody, and have a very high success rate. They lay a small tinted egg daily during their laying season. On average they will lay up to a total of 120 eggs a year. American game chickens are good fliers and very hardy. The cockerels will fight to the death if left with one another and as such they must be separated early in life.

## Indian

The Indian game hen lays up to 80 small light brown eggs per year. Their hardy feathers make them cold hardy though they prefer mild weather. They are best known for their meat qualities and are a stout substantially-sized chicken. It was once quite common to breed Indian game, the Sussex and Dorking to provide a particularly large table bird. A sensible and confident bird, Indian game chickens are easily tamed. Due to their body contours they find it difficult to fully preen themselves and have increased vulnerability to mites and lice.

## Modern English

These chickens are elegant and smaller than their game counterparts. English game chickens stand tall and are known for their curiosity. As they enjoy flying and climbing, it is necessary to ensure the garden is secure to keep them from harm. While they can tolerate very warm temperatures, they do not thrive in the cold. They are slow to mature, but when they do they are productive layers over a very short season. The Modern English game hen will lay up to 60 small white eggs per a year.

# Summing Up

- Chickens come in almost every size, shape and colour imaginable. Take your time and decide which breed is best suited to your needs.

- Light breeds will use less feed per egg than heavier breeds. However, they are more vulnerable to predators.

- Heavy breeds consume a lot of feed and may produce fewer larger eggs. This is due to a long history of selecting birds for the table.

- Hybrids are commercial cross breeds. They are egg laying machines and have been selected to have a calm disposition.

- If you have limited space, bantams are an excellent solution. What they lack in size, they make up for in personality.

- Rehoming an ex-battery hen can be a very positive experience. However, they are not guaranteed layers, and will require special care initially.

- Game breeds were originally bred for cock fights. Now they are primarily bred for show. While beautiful, they are not reliable egg layers.

# Chapter Three

# Feeding and Nutrition

## Basic anatomy

Understanding your chicken's digestive system will help you properly nourish them and could save you money on unnecessary extras. Knowing what is normal and what is not will will help you recognise when something is wrong and to have a better understanding of what to do.

## Beak

A chicken begins digesting its food in the beak. They produce saliva which they mix with their food to make swallowing easier. A chicken has a tongue but no human-like teeth.

## Crop

Once swallowed, food and water is stored in the crop. The crop is a little pocket at the base of the neck which allows birds to eat large quantities of food quickly. Food and water is stored in the crop until the stomach is ready for more food. As the crop empties it begins to send hunger signals to the chicken to begin eating again.

## Proventriculus

A chicken's stomach is called a proventriculus and breaks down the food with enzymes. This is very similar to a human stomach, the exception is that the food has yet to be ground up.

## Gizzard

Food then passes on to the gizzard, which is made up of two strong muscles. Chickens eat grit and gravel and store it in their gizzard to grind up their food. The grit and gravel is slowly broken into smaller pieces over time and is passed with the undigested food.

## Small intestine

From the gizzard, the food is passed through the duodenal loop and into the small intestine where most of the nutrient absorption occurs.

## Caeca

Any remaining undigested food ferments and is subject to microbial breakdown in the caeca.

## Large intestine

The large intestine is actually very small in chickens and absorbs more water.

## Cloaca

This is often called a vent and is responsible for all the chicken's elimination needs: faeces, urine, seminal fluid and eggs.

Chickens within a flock will know how much and when they eat. Most chickens will eat two large meals a day at first light and in the late evening. Throughout the day they will snack every fifteen minutes or so. Young birds will digest their food very quickly. A chick will have its food pass from beak to cloaca in just four hours. A laying hen will average around eight hours, and a broody hen's digestion will slow down to around twelve hours for completion. If you are raising chicks it is important to have food freely available for just this reason.

'The digestive system of poultry is quite different from other animals as they lack teeth.'
Dr. Deepa, Assistant Professor at the Centre for Advanced Studies in Poultry Science.

# What to feed your chickens

Chickens can only store around 100g of food in their crop at a time. This is roughly a handful or about the size of an egg. If you choose to provide food freely, monitor your hens to ensure none are growing fat. A fat hen will lay fewer eggs and be prone to numerous health complaints. Chickens are not allowed to be fed any feed containing mammalian or avian derived protein. This is important as many kind people may offer advice such as how extra protein is beneficial at different stages of a chicken's life. It is now advised not to feed chickens animal products in order to prevent the spread of disease and illness. This is not the case with dairy. Chickens can and do enjoy treats such as cheese and yogurt.

## Commercial chicken feed

Many chickens are fed on packaged ground feeds. These are available in all garden stores, pet stores and online. The benefits of choosing commercial chicken feed is that they already have exactly the correct balance of minerals and nutrients for a healthy chicken.

Chickens need to start on chick starter crumb. This feed is ground up quite small to allow young chicks to feed easily. It should be fed from day one until their sixth week. Chick crumb is available medicated or unmedicated. The medicated crumb contains ACS (Anti-Coccidiostat) to prevent toxidiosis. Toxidosis will be discussed further in chapter 6.

From six weeks until sixteen weeks of age, chickens are offered growers pellets. Growers pellets contain a higher protein level than chick crumb to allow chickens to produce feathers and support them during a period of heavy growth.

For laying hens, laying pellets or layers mash have been specially designed to support a hen to produce eggs and maintain her own health. Pellets and mash are the same food in different forms. Pellets are great for fussy chickens and will ensure they eat all their vitamins. Mash can be given to slow a greedy hen down as it takes longer to eat. You can add warm water to mash to make hot cereal feed to warm your chickens in the winter.

'A fat hen will lay fewer eggs and be prone to numerous health complaints.'

Battery hens have special dietary needs and thrive best on pellets designed to support them. Ex-bat crumbs are specially designed to encourage feather growth and replenish chickens after having worked hard in a commercial setting.

## Mixing your own

There are many reasons why those raising chickens choose to mix their own feed. Some do it because they believe ground grains lose their nutritional value and that chickens receive the best from their food when it is whole and fresh. Others do it because they feel their chickens enjoy eating a diet rich in textures and flavours. The immediate benefit from mixing your own feed is the cost. Not only can you mix your feed from inexpensive local producers, but there is less waste. Chickens will spread their feed around as they scratch. With commercial pellets the feed quickly dissolves and becomes inedible. Wholegrains will either be eaten or spread around in the chicken run to be eaten later.

## Should I buy organic?

Organic feeds are readily available and affordable. There are strict guidelines that regulate organic feed. Many people who choose organic feed do so to either to reduce the environmental impact of food production or to reduce the number of chemical their animals, and subsequently themselves, are exposed to.

Organic feed is ideal, however it is important to make your choice based on an occasionally unideal world. Most of the time chicken keepers will unanimously agree that organic is best for bird and human. However, whether you are keeping your chickens in a confined space or loose in a field, you may decide that medicated feed will help to ensure their long-term health and wellbeing.

Organic feed is produced by farms who work using the following principles:

▪ No GMO (genetically modified organisms), chemical fertilisers, pesticides or additives

- Raising livestock ethically by meeting their behavioural, health and psychological needs

- Respecting the natural cycles from soil, plant and animal

- Using compost to recycle nutrients

- Protecting and encouraging biodiversity

- Minimising pollution and waste

- Creating and expanding ecologically responsible production, processing and distribution channels

- Keeping processing to a minimum

## Foraging

Chickens are excellent foragers. They love to graze on a variety of plants and will spend hours each day searching out bugs and insects. In the wild a chicken would spend up to 60% of its time pecking the ground regardless of actual hunger. Chickens enjoy foraging beneath trees, bushes and around walls. They will avoid open fields and large empty spaces.

It is possible that chickens who are allowed to forage and eat a natural and varied diet may produce eggs richer in many vitamins and minerals. It is suggested by the Soil Association that similar to humans, chickens digest and absorb their nutrients better when they eat a varied diet and are not relying solely on a multivitamin tablet.

'The nutritional needs of each chicken will vary depending on their age, breed and their environment.'

## Vital nutrients

The nutritional needs of each chicken will vary depending on their age, breed and their environment. The average laying hen will metabolise around 1,300 calories per day.

A hen's diet should include the following:

- Protein – 16-18%

- Calcium – 3.75%

- Oil and fats – 4.0%
- Fibre – 6.0%
- Vitamin A – 7,500 iu/kg
- Vitamin D – 3,000 iu/kg

# Supplements

## Calcium

Eggshells are primarily made up of calcium carbonate. As such, laying hens need calcium to produce strong eggshells. Older hens require a little more calcium than younger ones do. In hot weather chickens will eat less and need a little extra calcium.

'Cod liver oil is rich in vitamin D and chickens love it.'

Calcium can be offered as oyster shells and ground up limestone. These are readily available from anywhere selling chicken feed. Do not buy dolomite limestone as this is harmful.

## Vitamin D

In order to properly absorb calcium and phosphorus, chickens need vitamin D. Most feeds have sufficient vitamin D during the summer months when the chickens are getting plenty of sunlight. During the short winter months offering them a little extra will ensure their long-term health. Cod liver oil is rich in vitamin D and chickens love it.

## Grit

Grit is important for a chicken to properly digest their feed. It is sold as large bags of small pebbles and should always be made available. If your chickens are allowed to free range it is not necessary to provide grit, unless your birds are short of space. Chickens will peck at the ground and unearth all kinds of tiny pebbles. If your free-ranging chickens appear to be having digestive upset, you can keep grit on hand as a preventative measure.

## Riboflavin

Riboflavin is a B vitamin and has been found to be deficient in many of the commercial feeds. This is not a problem for laying hens themselves. A deficiency of riboflavin causes early embryo death during incubation. If you would like to hatch chicks from your hen's eggs, then offer a supplement. Riboflavin can be found in leafy green vegetables, liver, yeast and dairy products.

## Vitamin E

This vitamin nurtures the chicken's immune system and helps to stave off disease. Vitamin E is found in wholegrains, wheat germ oil, and fresh greens.

## Apple cider vinegar

Due to its acidity, apple cider vinegar acts as a mild antiseptic. It is believed to kill off numerous bacteria that cause disease in chickens. In addition it helps with digestion and may help to prevent worms. Apple cider vinegar is rich in vitamins and minerals and can be added to drinking water. Only add apple cider vinegar to a plastic drinker and not to metal ones.

'A laying hen will drink up to 500ml of water every day.'

# Water

A laying hen will drink up to 500ml of water every day. Chickens drink little and often, by taking a sip and then looking up at the sky to swallow. If a laying hen is unable to access water for over 24 hours, she will take time to recover and cease laying for a period.

Water is primarily a concern in winter, and drinkers need to be checked regularly to ensure they have not frozen.

## Can I feed my chickens leftovers?

In Britain it is the law that you cannot feed domestic kitchen scraps to chickens. This is due to the potential risk of contamination and the spread of disease. Basically, if a chicken is fed leftover meats or food that have gone off it may result in a chicken carrying an illness. The most common illness is salmonella which is a bacteria that attacks the stomach and intestines. Diarrhoea, stomach cramps, nausea and fever are all common symptoms. Salmonella is a particular threat to pregnant women and those with weaker immune systems due to the risk of complications.

You can still offer your hens treats by the means of anything grown in your garden. They can have raw vegetable peelings, such as carrot tops. Do not feed raw potatoes to hens, as they are toxic.

'In Britain it is the law that you cannot feed domestic kitchen scraps to chickens. This is due to the potential risk of contamination and the spread of disease.'

# Summing Up

- Feeding your chickens a balanced diet will ensure a steady supply of eggs and ensure the chickens' long-term health.

- Chickens tend to eat two large meals a day and store up to 100g of food in their crop.

- Commercial chicken feeds offer simple and balanced nutrition for different age groups. These can be bought as mash or pellets.

- When mixing your feed it is important to ensure your chickens are getting the right balance of nutrients.

- Organic feeds are a great way to reduce the volume of chemicals and medications your chickens are receiving and to support sustainable farming methods.

- Chickens need the opportunity to forage. They are beak-oriented creatures who love bug-hunting and exploring their environment.

- Ensuring your chickens have enough calcium will allow them to produce strong eggshells.

- Chickens do not have teeth. They require grit to help them break down their food.

- Apple cider vinegar is a natural way to prevent chickens from worms, and to add extra vitamins and minerals.

- It is against the law to feed kitchen waste to chickens due to the risk of salmonella infection.

# Chapter Four

# Preparing For Your Chickens

## Housing

Housing chickens is certainly an area of debate. Commercial flat-packed chicken houses can be bought from almost anywhere. Often these chicken houses are categorised by how many chickens they can hold. Be cautious when buying a chicken house. Technically, the space required to properly house a chicken is set at 12 inches squared per chicken. Just consider that for a moment. That does not afford them very much room for movement. Should you purchase one of these tiny chicken houses and fill it to capacity, you will need to clean it out thoroughly every single day. The air will become very stale and filled with ammonia, and your hens may become poorly. Ideally, each chicken should be given 36 to 60 inches squared each.

'Ideally, each chicken should be given 36 to 60 inches squared each.'

## How to decide how big a house your chickens need

### How many chickens do you intend to keep?

If possible, consider a chicken house that is slightly larger than your initial needs. It is very easy to start expanding a flock. Should you hatch eggs, or bring home a new hen, then you will then have the room without crowding your existing birds.

## What breed are your chickens?

Bantams require far less space than large fowl. If you have a mix of breeds it is better to use the largest chicken as your guide to estimate space requirements.

## Are they free ranging?

Chickens will require less housing space the more area they have available to them outdoors. If your chickens are free ranging, then they can make do with less individual area.

A chicken house does not need to be fancy. You can convert an old shed, or buy one ready made. In order to decide what kind would best suit your needs, it may be worth visiting a few local farms. Have a look at the housing choices they have made and do not hesitate to ask questions. Chicken keepers are a friendly bunch, and will happily talk about chickens for as long as you will listen.

'A chicken house does not need to be fancy. You can convert an old shed, or buy one ready made.'

# Nest boxes

For every three hens you keep it is important to provide one nest box. If you keep twelve chickens you will require at least four nest boxes. A hen prefers to lay her eggs in a dark, quiet place. If the nest box is too light she will soil the nest box and you will have dirty eggs. If the nest box has a draught or is noisy, you will find she lays her eggs anywhere in the garden, which makes them difficult to collect. It also leaves a hen vulnerable to predators. Each nesting box needs to be just big enough to hold one hen. A square of around 18 inches is perfect and should sit slightly off the floor. Keeping the top closed off to prevent the chickens roosting above the nest boxes and subsequently soiling them is important. Nest boxes do not need to be perfect. A milk crate on its side is perfect. Hens will happily nest in laundry baskets, washing-up tubs, and even a three-gallon bucket!

# Perches

Each chicken needs twelve inches of perching space. The perch should be about one and a half inches square with the top edges rounded down. If the perch is too round or too small the chickens could develop foot problems. The perch should be placed between 6 and 18 inches off the ground. Generally, it is best to put your perch a little bit higher than your nest boxes. Otherwise your chickens may prefer to sleep in there. If you have heavy breed chickens you will need to put your perches quite low to enable the birds to alight and dismount without injuring themselves.

# Bedding

There are a many bedding options available which are safe to use with poultry. Choose a bedding for your chickens that is readily available, and suits your budget and cleaning routine.

'For every three hens you keep it is important to provide one nest box.'

## Wood shavings

Dust-extracted wood shavings are relatively cheap and are easily available. The shavings are soft and insulating. Highly absorbent, they will reduce the ammonia in the air to control odour and prevent the development of respiratory illnesses.

It is important not to use shavings for chicks as they will eat them and this could cause fatalities. In addition, wood shavings should be from soft woods, as hard woods can contain fungi and moulds which can cause respiratory problems.

## Auboise

This bedding is made from hemp and is very popular. With natural qualities which repel flies and provided good insulation, it is also dust free and very absorbent. Auboise decomposes quickly, which makes it ideal to add to your compost. Auboise is a more expensive option and is primarily available to purchase in large quantities.

### Shredded paper

Shredded paper can be used as bedding but will have to be changed frequently. It is not very absorbent or comfortable. If it is used in generous quantities it can be adapted to suit a chicken's needs.

### Chopped cardboard

Chopped cardboard, or Ecobed, is more absorbent than shredded paper. It is made from recycled cardboard and composts very quickly. This may be a good option if you have a steady supply of cardboard from a pre-existing source. Chopped cardboard may not be an ideal option for those wishing to use the deep litter method of hen house management.

'Straw and hay are not recommended for use as bedding. They become damp very easily and will grow fungal spores that cause aspergillosis.'

### Straw and hay

Straw and hay are not recommended for use as bedding. They become damp very easily and will grow fungal spores that cause aspergillosis. They are also believed to be superior breeding grounds for lice and mites.

# Securing the garden and protecting your chickens

Some cockerels are great bodyguards. They keep their hens safe and will take on anything that comes their way. Others are pretty cowardly and will be the first ones to high tail it out at the first signs of trouble. Regardless of whether you have a cockerel or not, there are some tried and tested ways of keeping your chickens safe from other animals.

In the UK the two primary predators for urban chickens are foxes and rats. Badgers, dogs, cats, birds of prey, pine martens and weasels can also be a problem. The first and most effective way of protecting your hens from predators is to lock them up in a secure hen house at night. Some animals, such as badgers, are strong and with determination, can break into a wooden coop. Building a strong home that is regularly checked for weak spots will ensure each morning you have the same number of hens as the night before. If possible, build your hen house up off the ground. Having nest boxes and perches well placed will also prevent other animals from easily accessing your sleeping hens or their eggs.

Unfortunately, predators will strike during the daylight hours as well as at night. It is important to keep your chickens protected while out free ranging. Chickens are sensitive creatures, and the stress of being chased by a dog is enough to put a hen off lay.

The best way to keep your chickens safe is to only let them completely loose in the garden when you are available to supervise. Unless you are very dedicated, it is very difficult to thoroughly enclose an entire garden. When you are not able to be there to watch over your chickens keep them in a movable run. A chicken run is often made from a wooden frame covered over in chicken wire. You can either build your own, or purchase a ready-made kit from almost any pet or garden store. A large rabbit or guinea pig run would be more than acceptable for a trio of hens.

There are a wide variety of products available for deterring predators. Foxwatch emits an ultrasonic sound that keeps foxes away. This device is quite popular and is said to be fairly effective.

'In the UK the two primary predators for urban chickens are foxes and rats.'

## Tasty treat or tummy ache?

One crucial part of securing your garden is to identify and remove any poisonous plants your chickens may come in contact with. If you cannot or do not want to remove them, then it will be important to ensure suitable fencing is in place. Most chickens will avoid them, however, young and greedy birds may forage on a little of everything.

**Common plants that are toxic to poultry:**

▦ Alfalfa

▦ Bryony

▦ Daffodil

▦ Delphinium

- Eggplant
- Elderberry
- Fern
- Foxglove
- Holly
- Honeysuckle
- Horse chestnut
- Horse radish
- Hyacinth
- Hydrangea
- Iris
- Ivy
- Laburnum
- Laurel
- Lilly of the valley
- Mistletoe
- Nightshade
- Ragwort
- Rhododendron
- Rhubarb
- St John's wort
- Tomato leaves
- Tulip
- Wild onion
- Wisteria

'One crucial part of securing your garden is to identify and remove any poisonous plants your chickens may come in contact with.'

This list is not complete. There are over one hundred and fifty plants listed as toxic to poultry and as such only the most common found in UK gardens have been listed. For a comprehensive list please visit The Poultry Club Of Great Britain's website, see the help list for details.

# Drinkers

There are as many kinds of drinker as there are glass tumbler. You could choose to offer your hens water from a regular bowl, however the water will quickly become contaminated with dirt and faeces. Chickens have a tendency to leave their droppings in water if given the opportunity.

Drinkers are designed to hold between one and four gallons of water. The choice of size will depend on how many chickens you are keeping. Water needs to be refreshed every day regardless of how much water is remaining.

Two designs currently rule the poultry drinker market: automatic bell drinkers and tripods.

## Bell drinkers

Bell drinkers are the cheap and cheerful option. They keep the water clean and are ideal for large numbers of chickens. The downfall to the bell drinker is its clumsy filling technique. The water storage jug must be filled upside down and then have the bottom fitted, before tipping the drinker right side up. This is can be quite cumbersome.

## Tripods

Tripod drinkers are are more expensive and prove popular with those who have tried them. This drinker uses a ball valve to fill a small dish with water from a larger tank. The tank is filled from the top and is significantly easier to manage should you suffer from back or joint pain. The opening for filling tripods tends to be quite small. Filling a tripod becomes a lot easier if you use a funnel.

'Water needs to be refreshed every day regardless of how much water is remaining.'

# Feeders

Feeders are designed to keep chickens from soiling in their food. When choosing a feeder try to ensure each chicken will have four inches of space to eat comfortably and to avoid bullying. Ideally, the feeder should be lifted off the ground to around the chickens' neck height. This will vary if you have younger chicks as well. The purpose of keeping the feeder off the ground is to reduce contamination and to ensure that rats and other pests are unable to easily access the feed.

# Summing Up

■ Choose a house for your chickens that can accommodate all of your birds comfortably. A general rule of thumb is at least 12 inches per chicken.

■ Ensure your chicken house has a comfortable perch and at least one nest box for every three hens.

■ Decide on a bedding that is affordable, readily available, and suits your maintenance style. Wood shavings or Auboise will insulate your hen house well, while providing great moisture absorption.

■ Check and repair fencing to ensure your garden is predator proof. If this is not possible build an enclosed chicken run.

■ Identify your garden plants. There are many common garden plants that are toxic to chickens.

# Chapter Five

# Purchasing Your Chickens

## How many chickens?

Chickens are social creatures. They have gentle hearts and often fail to thrive if left on their own. It is recommended to keep a minimum of three chickens to ensure that when one dies there is a companion to help through the grieving process. The first consideration is space. How much space do you have for your chickens? Each chicken should have at least 12 square inches of space within their house, and 36 inches squared of space to run. This is the bare minimum and every chicken aspires to as much open space as possible.

Eggs tend to be the next major consideration. How many eggs does your family eat in a given week? Three hens will, during their peak laying years, lay an average of two eggs a day. Once you have decided how many eggs you would like it is important to remember chickens will decrease the eggs they lay by around 10% every year after their second year. It may be that you decide to introduce new hens as the older ones stop laying. As chickens will live between five and ten years, it is worth considering how your flock may look a few years down the road.

## What age to purchase?

### Point of lay

The easiest age to purchase chickens is at point of lay. Point of lay means a chicken that is around 20 weeks old. All the hard work of rearing the chicks has been done and the chicken is now ready to begin laying eggs. The downside

'It is recommended to keep a minimum of three chicken to ensure that when one dies there is a companion to help through the grieving process.'

to purchasing point of lay hens is that they are the most expensive. The upheaval of moving house will also disrupt the chicken and as such it may be a week or two before she settle in to producing eggs.

## Pullet

A hen between the age of eight weeks up to one year old is called a pullet. However, when purchasing a hen before the point of lay, she will often be referred to as a pullet. Younger hens tend to be cheaper than point of lay hens and will be sexed. Many breeders are all too happy to rehome chickens early as this saves them feeding and housing them. This can be an ideal way to save a little bit of money without coming home with a half dozen cockerels.

'The easiest age to purchase chickens is at point of lay. Point of lay means a chicken that is around 20 weeks old.'

## Chicks

Chicks tend to be sold as day olds. They are rarely just a day old and can be up to two weeks old. Chicks will require vigilant care and heat until they are fully feathered. If you have not reared chicks before this can be an exciting adventure, albeit lots of work. Chicks are fragile creatures but should you choose to rear your own you will find them exceptionally friendly and easy to handle throughout their life. Chicks, unless purchased from an autosexing breed, will have a mix of both genders. It is important to consider what you wish to do with three of four cockerels should you find them in your care.

## Ex-bats

If you are not concerned about egg production and are looking for a deserving pet, an ex-bat hen may be just the bird for you. Ex-bats are not for the faint-hearted, they often come home missing feathers, and looking quite poor. With the right care many go on to thrive. However, these hens have been bred for their particularly docile nature and can make excellent pets for children.

# Where to buy chickens?

## Breeders

A well-reputed breeder will always be your safest place to purchase chickens. They will have vaccinated their flocks and tended their breeding lines well. Ask around and see if anyone can recommend a local breeder. Allotments and feed stores will often advertise and offer the opportunity to ask around. Otherwise, have a look online as many breeds have their own club.

## Poultry shows

Attending a poultry show will allow you to see the very best of breed standards. Most poultry shows will have sale pens where breeders can sell stock from their show birds. These chickens will be the cream of the crop and you can expect high quality. It does deserve mentioning that chickens have been bred for several purposes throughout their domestication. Breeders tend to breed for utility, which will result in regular egg laying. However, chickens bred for show will be selected for their beautiful plumage. It is generally accepted that show lines are not as productive as utility lines.

'Chicks will require vigilant care and heat until they are fully feathered.'

## Poultry auctions

Auctions are becoming more popular and are worth a visit. There will be a wide variety of chickens on offer and it will provide the opportunity to make contact with a lot of people who keep chickens.

When buying from auction it is important to know exactly what you are looking for. Spotting an ill chicken is not always easy as chickens tend to be quite stoic about ailments.

## Private ads

Private ads can be found online or in newspapers. Here you will find chickens being sold by hobby breeders who have done their very best to ensure a good start for your chickens. It is important to go and have a look without commitment. Quality can vary dramatically within a specific breed and sometimes poor breeding can result in lines being reproduced that should not have been.

# Rehoming ex-battery hens

It is increasingly popular to rehome ex-battery hens. Commercial laying hens are almost always a hybrid breed. Typically, the hens will be Hylines, Goldlines or ISAS. They are around seventy weeks old when they are rehomed. This is the age at which they are no longer commercially viable due to the decrease in their egg production. These breeds are bred for their gentle nature which makes them excellent pets.

Chickens coming from a commercial cage environment are going to experience far greater stress while moving house than a chicken reared by a hobby breeder. It is crucial that they receive extra support during their first few weeks in their new home.

These hens will need to be kept separate from any other chickens you have for two or three weeks. Until now they have not had the room to exercise and will be physically unfit. Many will have feather loss, and subsequently experience poor self-esteem. Hens need to be able to stand up for themselves or they will be bullied. These hens tend to have large, pale and floppy combs due to the heat they experienced in their crowded accommodation. The comb will become small and red with time. Until the comb has shrunk and darkened, other chickens may try to peck and grab hold of it. It can be helpful to apply petroleum jelly to the comb to prevent other chickens being able to grab hold.

If you are interested in rehoming ex-bats please visit the British Hen Welfare Trust at www.bhwt.org.uk. Also see the help list for information. They help with rehoming commercial laying hens as well as providing support and information for those caring for ex-battery hens.

## Hatching eggs

Watching your own eggs pip, unzip and become a fluffy little chick is a great joy. Hatching eggs can be bought from most breeders, or you can collect from your own chickens, provided you have a cockerel. Hatching eggs will require a broody hen or an incubator. There is a more about hatching eggs in chapter 8.

# Handling and transporting

Chickens do not like moving house. They loathe car rides, and do not like going in boxes. The stress they undergo is probably something like how humans feel about trips to the dentist. To ensure their journey goes smoothly, take the time to prepare everything in advance. Prepare the chicken house and bedding the day before your chickens are to come home. Then just prior to setting off, put out their food and water. This way you can unload your chickens and then leave them to settle in uninterrupted.

'According to the British Hen Welfare Trust, there are approximately 16 million caged hens woking for the commercial egg industry for the UK.'

To carry your chickens from the breeder to your home you could buy bird transport boxes. These are specially designed and very expensive for a single trip. You can use a large cardboard box or an appropriately sized dog crate. Take in to account the weather and length of the journey. Ensure there is adequate bedding, especially if it is cold, and that there are plenty of air holes. Try to use a bedding material, like shavings that will provide traction and to absorb moisture. If you use a cardboard box, line the bottom beneath the bedding with plastic. Chickens will soil the box and there is a risk the bottom could fall out. As an additional caution reseal the bottom of the box with strong packing tape. The last thing you will want is for the bottom to come apart between the car and the hen house.

If you have plenty of boxes, each chicken can be transported individually. However, should you have a box large enough, hens will remain calm and quiet through the duration of their journey if they are allowed to remain together. Secure the top of the box or you will have chickens escaping while you are navigating down the motorway!

Do not stop along the journey home. It is important to get the chickens to their new home quickly. If it is very hot out, roll the windows down, or turn on the air conditioning. Hens overheat quickly, and will become increasingly stressed.

## Picking up a chicken

To pick up a chicken, place your hands over each wing and around the chicken's rib cage. Lift the chicken up with a firm but gentle hold. Chickens are quite delicate and will flap their wings the moment their feet leave the ground. In order to protect yourself and the chicken from injury it is important to secure their wings in the palm of your hand. Chickens settle quickly when hugged up against your chest and are carried easily in this position.

## After dark

Chickens become very still after dark. If you need to catch a hen who is not used to handling then go into the hen house just after dark. Use a torch to help you find the chicken you are looking for and collect her with the light turned off.

'Chickens settle quickly when hugged up against your chest and are carried easily in this position.'

# Summing Up

- Purchase no less than three chickens to ensure they have company should one chicken become ill and pass away.

- Purchasing a chicken at point of lay is the easiest way to start. The hard work of hatching and rearing the chicken has already been done.

- For best value for money buy young pullets.

- Chicks are a lot of work. They need chick-proof housing and lots of heat.

- Ex-battery hens can make rewarding pets but need extra tender loving care.

- Poultry shows are a great place to learn more about the breeds you are interested in.

- Prepare your chickens' house and run in advance of collecting them to ensure their first day home is as stress free as possible.

- When picking up a chicken secure their wings on both sides and keep them close to your body.

# Chapter Six

## Health

## Cleanliness

Prevention is the most important aspect of caring for your chickens' health. It is far easier to prevent illness from striking, than it is to remedy. Keeping your chicken house and run clean is the best way to ensure your chickens have a long and healthy life.

### Chicken house cleaning basics

Once a day go in and scoop out any visible faeces and throw it in the compost. Take a minute to inspect the house and clean out any wet bedding.

Once a week take all the chickens out of the house and lock them outside. Remove all bedding and discard into the compost. Scrub the interior with a solution of vinegar and water, and rinse well. Any dirt or faeces that is stuck on can be easily lifted using a putty knife.

After the house is cleaned out spray the floor, ceiling, nest boxes, walls and perches with Poultry Shield or a similar product. Poultry Shield is used to kill and prevent red mite infestation.

Leave the chicken house to dry. Once all the surfaces are dry, dust all surfaces with food grade diatomaceous earth. Diatomaceous earth is a natural and safe way to keep your chicken house free from lice, mites and fleas.

Finally, add fresh bedding back into the chicken house. Open the door and allow the chickens to come in and inspect your handiwork.

'It is far easier to prevent illness from striking, than it is to remedy.'

# Mites and lice

Mites and lice are small creatures that can cause big problems. Once they have happily installed themselves in your hen house it is very difficult to get rid of them completely. Left untreated, an infestation will dramatically affect the health of your flock. Egg production will drop, pale combs and wattles plus feather loss will develop, and it can lead to death.

Mites appear as little moving specks. They are technically arachnids and have eight legs. Mites feed on the blood of chickens, and typically come out at night. During the day, the most common, red poultry mite, will hide in cracks and crevices in the chicken house. Chicken mites can and will bite humans. As they are not active during the day most people will not be bitten by them. These bites may be painful and will cause itching.

Another mite to be aware of is the scaly leg mite. This is a very tiny mite that burrows under the scales of a chicken's legs. The first symptom of scaly leg mites tends to be a flaky and brittle look to the leg skin. If left untreated it will progress to lesions, swelling, and can cripple a chicken. Scaly leg mites are most common in older chickens. This can be treated by rubbing petroleum jelly on the chicken's legs every day for two weeks.

Poultry lice are tiny wingless insects with a light brown body. They feed on the chicken's dry skin scales, scabs and part of the feathers. If lice find the skin to be broken, they will take the opportunity to feed on the chicken's blood. Poultry lice do not transfer to humans.

There are a variety of powders and sprays available to treat mites and lice. It is important to follow the directions carefully and only use approved products for poultry. Another preventative measure is to put diatomaceous earth in the hens dust bath. The hens will cover themselves and kill any parasites the diatomaceous earth comes in contact with.

> 'Mites and lice are small creatures that can cause big problems. Once they have happily installed themselves in your hen house it is very difficult to get rid of them completely.'

# Laying problems

Every now and again a chicken may run into troubles while laying an egg or stop laying all together. It is important to know when they simply need good food and patience, and when to step in and help.

# Egg bound

A hen becomes egg bound when her egg becomes stuck in her vent. This is serious and requires immediate attention. Toxic shock will set in and the chicken will die within 48 hours.

New layers may sometimes become egg bound as their body is learning to lay. Hens at peak lay may become egg bound when they have produced a particularly large egg. Hens are most at risk of becoming egg bound if they are overweight, underweight or have low calcium levels.

Symptoms of an egg bound hen are as follows:

- Fluffed up feathers
- Refuses food and water
- Appears distressed and in pain
- Strains without result
- Rapid or laboured breathing
- Found on the hen house floor
- Her vent is hot, swollen and red
- Unable to pass faeces

Should your chicken become egg bound you need to lubricate the hen's vent to free the egg. Using a lubricant or vegetable oil, insert your finger into the hen's vent and gently rub the abdomen to ease the egg out. It is very important to avoid causing cuts or tears which can become infected. Wash your hands, trim your nails and use soft latex gloves.

Do not try to break the egg and remove it in pieces. This can cause septicaemia as the eggshell pieces may cut the oviduct.

As a last resort a hen may be helped by being rested in a warm bath for a few minutes to relax and allow the egg to shift.

If you are unsure if your hen is egg bound you can consult your veterinarian. An X-ray is a valuable tool in determining the exact problem. In severe cases a complete hysterectomy is necessary to save the chicken.

'A hen becomes egg bound when her egg becomes stuck in her vent. Hens are most at risk of becoming egg bound if they are overweight, underweight or have low calcium levels.'

## Prolapse

Prolapse occurs when the lower section of a hen's oviduct comes out of the vent. If your chicken develops a prolapse the first thing to do is to separate them from the other chickens. This will ensure that the prolapse is not torn or pecked at.

- Clean the exposed oviduct.
- Gently replace the prolapsed tissue manually.
- Apply haemorrhoid ointment to reduce swelling.
- Offer the hen vitamins and electrolytes to help her rebalance her body.
- Give antibiotics if the oviduct has been pecked, or is dirty.

## Eating their eggs

'Once hens find out what a delicious and tasty treat they produce, they will continue to consume their own eggs. It is important to break this habit early as it becomes harder to fix the longer it goes on.'

If an eggs breaks in the hen house the odds are good that the chickens will eat it. Once hens find out what a delicious and tasty treat they produce, they will continue to consume their own eggs. It is important to break this habit early as it becomes harder to fix the longer it goes on.

Ideally, it is best to prevent an egg breaking in the first place.

What can I do to prevent eggs breaking?

- Ensure the hens have plenty of calcium to keep the eggshells strong. Ground oyster shells are readily available for this purpose.
- Ensure you have enough nest boxes for your chickens and that the nest boxes are dark and have deep bedding.
- Try to collect your eggs early and frequently. The less time an egg spends with the hens, the less likely it will become damaged.

If your chickens start eating their eggs you can try to fool them by placing plastic eggs or golf balls in the nest. This may discourage them from trying to break open their eggs as these will not crack open.

Another method to discourage egg eating is to prick the ends of an egg and blow out the contents. Then using a syringe, fill the egg with mustard and chilli sauce. Hens should learn quickly that eggs do not taste good!

If one hen is very persistent, it may be wise to remove her from the group for a few days to break the habit and prevent her continuing to encourage the others in their behaviour.

## Why have my chickens stopped laying?

Do not worry if your chicken go off laying for a period. Declining daylight will discourage hens from producing eggs. In the winter, hens will cease laying until there is daylight for 12 continuous hours. Hens will moult once a year. As growing feathers and producing eggs are both full-time jobs, the hens will stop laying for a few weeks. Age and broodiness cause hens to go off laying, and are not cause for concern. There are some diseases that can cause egg production to stop. As well, poor diet and dehydration will cease egg production. If either are suspected they need to be remedied quickly.

# Digestive upset

Chickens will sometimes find and consume something which causes them stomach upset. If a chicken consumes food that has spoiled or gone mouldy they may become listless and stand off in a corner with their eyes closed. If one of your chickens develops a stomach ache remove her from the flock and keep her in a small pen. Ensure she is warm and has plenty of fresh water.

Occasionally chickens are affected by botulism. This starts off with stomach ache symptoms and develops into weakness and paralysis of the legs, wings and then neck. Sudden death is common. Botulism is caused by chickens developing a bacterial infection after consuming a decaying animal, plant waste or pond mud.

'In the winter, hens will cease laying until there is daylight for 12 continuous hours.'

# Common diseases

There are hundreds of illnesses chickens can become infected with, however most are exceptionally rare. Let's look at the five most common diseases and how to prevent them.

### Avian flu

This is the latest disease which has been making news headlines and causing panic. While the possibility of transmission of this flu is possible between birds to humans, it is important to remember it is a very rare disease and it is preventable with good hygiene. Equally, it is rare for domestic poultry to become infected. Avian flu is spread through body secretions of wild birds that are infected. Should your chicken become infected they will be dead within 48 hours. The chicken will exhibit lethargy, diarrhoea, breathing difficulties and dullness prior to quick onset of death. The only way to fully protect your chickens from avian flu is to keep them indoors at all times. If you choose to free range your chickens then ensure they are fed and watered indoors to prevent wild birds from contaminating their food and drink.

### Coccidiosis

This is a common and very contagious disease. It cannot be passed on to humans. When chickens peck at the ground they take in oocysts, tiny eggs laid in the faeces of birds infected with coccidiosis. Coccidiosis affects the intestines and causes chickens to become lethargic and experience dramatic weight loss. The chicken will be weak and keep their feathers fluffed up. There are medications you can buy to add to your drinkers should you suspect your flock has been infected. The easiest way to avoid a coccidiosis infection is by ensuring your chickens are fed medicated chicken feed as chicks.

### Marek's disease

Marek's disease is a severely infectious virus that attacks the chicken's nervous system. This is not transmittable to humans. Young stock is most at risk of death from Marek's disease. This disease tends to strike at around 12 weeks of age. This disease comes from the herpes virus, and once it strikes the possibility of recovery is almost non-existent. It is very important to keep all equipment clean to avoid passing on serious illness.

## Newcastle disease

This has also been known as fowl pest and can lead to a swift death in under 24 hours. It includes symptoms such as struggling and gasping for breath, discharge from the eyes and nose, a spreading paralysis throughout the body, and a change in dropping colour to green. Newcastle disease is very rare in Great Britain thanks to vaccination programmes. It is a highly infectious airborne disease and should infection be suspected it is important to notify Defra immediately. Newcastle disease will not be passed on to humans.

# Vaccines

Vaccines have come a long way over the last century and are tremendously important in the defense against disease and illness. Vaccines protect chickens from fatal diseases, disabling conditions, and diseases which cause health problems to their human caregivers, such as salmonella.

When you purchase your chickens always ask about their vaccination history. A reputable breeder will always vaccinate for Newcastle disease, Marek's disease and infectious bronchitis.

There is no standard set of vaccines that a back garden poultry keeper must use. It is entirely up to the individual chicken keeper. The vaccines required under the lion code are as follows: Marek's disease, avian pneumovirus, Newcastle disease, infectious bronchitis variants, infectious bursal disease (Gumboro disease) and salmonella. It is worth doing your research and considering vaccinating any chicks you hatch and rear yourself.

Most vaccines are straight forward and simple to use. They are easily obtainable from your local veterinarian. Some are simply added to the chickens' drinking water, others come as sprays, and a few require an injection. It is possible for anyone keeping chickens to purchase vaccines, however the major hurdle most chicken keepers face is quantity. The minimum dosage available for purchase is for one thousand birds. This results in a lot of

'When you purchase your chickens always ask about their vaccination history. A reputable breeder will always vaccinate for Newcastle disease, Marek's disease and infectious bronchitis.'

waste, and puts people off. If possible do try to form a group with other small flock holders in your area and vaccinate together. Not only will it reduce the cost, it will reduce the waste as well.

For further information on disease and prevention, the Department for Environment, Food & Rural Affairs (Defra) have a booklet available online called *Protecting Your Birds From the Risk of Disease 2012*. Go to www.defra. gov.uk, and visit the farm animals section. Under the poultry pages you will find a complete list of relevant leaflets for those raising chickens.

# Summing Up

- The best way to keep your chickens healthy is to keep their coop clean.

- A maintenance routine will keep jobs small and manageable while preventing problems from setting in.

- By spending a few minutes each day with your hens you will be able to identify signs of illness early.

- Vaccines are available for most common chicken diseases. These are a good front line defense against many fatal illnesses.

- When purchasing new stock always ask about their vaccination and health history.

# Chapter Seven

# Keeping Chickens Happy

## Free range

### What does free range mean?

In a commercial setting free range describes keeping chickens to a minimum of 36 inches squared per hen. In a home garden, chickens are typically kept either in a run or loose in the garden. Most chickens in home garden will be afforded far greater free ranging space then in a commercial setting. The main priority should always be to ensure that the chickens have the space to behave in a natural way, while ensuring their safety.

### Clipping wings

Deciding whether or not to clip your chickens' wings is a choice each chicken keeper must make for themselves. The major factor in making a decision should be the place the chickens are spending their days. If chickens are living only in an enclosed run, then there is little cause to clip their wings. If they are allowed to range in the garden then it may be necessary to clip their wings to prevent them flying away. This is a balancing act between the need to keep your birds home and in a safe environment, while also allowing a chicken its primary method of defense, flying away. If there are predators about it may be kinder to leave their wings intact. Most chickens will return to a familiar and favoured roost each night regardless of how far they have roamed.

To clip your chickens' wings, you must extend one wing out and trim the primary flight feathers. It is important to only trim the primary feathers as the others provide insulation. To see how far you should cut, you can shine a light

'In a commercial setting free range describes keeping chickens to a minimum of 36 inches squared per hen.'

through the feathers which will allow you to see where the blood vessels start in the feather shafts. A general rule of thumb is to clip away 5cm of feather. If you have any doubts, simply ask an experienced chicken keeper to show you how.

Chickens will regrow their feathers and as such wing clipping is not permanent. In a few months' time you can choose to re-clip the feathers, or if your chickens have learned to stay in their own territory you may no longer need to.

If you choose to clip your flock's wings it is important to only clip one wing. Otherwise the chickens will still be able to fly. If you have more than just a couple of chickens it may be helpful to clip only the right wing's feathers on all your chickens to enable you to remember who has been done and who has not even once new feathers have come in.

'If chickens are living only in an enclosed run, then there is little cause to clip their wings. If they are allowed to range in the garden then it may be necessary to clip their wings to prevent them flying away.'

## Deep litter method

Many chicken keepers do a complete chicken house clean out every week. The deep litter method is an alternative coop maintenance plan which is worth considering. The deep litter method starts by putting at least 6 inches of bedding into a clean chicken house. For this method hay and straw will not work. Wood shavings or hemp is the best because they are far more absorbent and will not grow mould.

As the floor becomes covered in dropping, you turn the bedding over and add fresh bedding. The bedding absorbs the smell and moisture. The bottom layer begins to break down and becomes compost. Meanwhile, the deep layers of bedding keep the chickens well insulated in the colder months. Once or twice a year, instead of every week, all the litter is removed and the chicken house is scrubbed out.

This method is great for the colder months of the year when keeping both the chickens and the chicken keeper warm and dry is the goal. Some chicken keepers do this year round and prefer it. Chickens do seem to prefer having deep bedding over shallow bedding and naturally turn their bedding over through scratching.

The deep litter method will not work if the chickens are overcrowded, or if the environment is excessively wet. The bedding should not smell. If an odour develops then the bedding must be cleared away and renewed.

To prevent red mites and other parasites from making a home in the deep bedding it is necessary to sprinkle diatomaceous earth each time you sprinkle on a new layer of bedding.

## Daily routine

Chickens like routine. They become stressed when they do not know what their day will bring and as such they will be happier if you have a daily routine.

First thing in the morning you will need to let your hens out of their house. Chickens like to go out and forage as soon as the sun shines as they have an empty crop. Chickens actually see the dawn as much as an hour earlier than we do, and will happily be out scratching the ground before we would declare it officially morning. If you work shifts or do not wish to go out early in the morning, you can purchase an automatic door opener and set it on a timer. These are relatively inexpensive and can be programmed to close the door at night.

Next, empty and clean out drink and feed containers and refill with fresh water and food. Stop for a few minutes and just watch your chickens. It is easy to forget to stand still. This can be the most valuable time you can give your chickens. By taking the time to watch them, you will become familiar with their daily habits and rituals. This is the best way for you to monitor the health of your chickens.

Mid-morning the chickens will have finished laying their eggs and they are ready for collection. While collecting the eggs, ensure the nesting boxes are clean and have sufficient bedding.

In the evenings the chickens need to be put to bed. Either by means of an automated door or by going out, bidding them goodnight and closing the door personally. Some young hens do not automatically learn to perch on their own. If you are closing the chicken house at night it may be helpful to stand any hens that are asleep on the ground on their perch. Soon they will perch on their own and their foot and leg health will be significantly better for it.

'Chickens like routine. They become stressed when they do not know what their day will bring and as such they will be happier if you have a daily routine.'

# Seasonal tips

Throughout the year your chickens' needs may change and vary.

## In the winter

- Keep their water from freezing. When the temperature starts to dip it is not uncommon to come outside in the morning and find the drinker frozen. Purchase a spare drinker and then you can rotate them. Chickens appreciate a warm drink almost as much as their human caregivers. Fill the drinker with warm, body temperature water. This will keep the water from freezing as quickly and will help the chickens keep warm.

- Collect your eggs frequently to prevent them freezing and cracking. Egg production tends to decrease which can make it hard to stay in the habit of vigilantly checking for eggs.

- If you wish to keep your hens in lay then install a light in the chicken house and turn it on to lengthen the daylight hours.

- Do not limit feed in the winter. During the summer months chickens will happily forage and find a great deal of their own food. In the winter they will be using a lot of calories to keep warm. To ensure their health it is important to keep their food containers full.

- Try to prevent draughts. If possible, position your hen house so that it is out of prevailing winds. A tarp or plastic sheeting can be affixed to one side of their run to provide a wind block. This will go a long way to reducing their calorie consumption and ability to get out of the chicken house to stretch their legs.

- If your chickens have an enclosed run, put a roof over the top. This will keep the soil from becoming a mud pit which can affect a chicken's feet.

## In the summer

Chickens can become very stressed and ill from the heat. Hens that have become overly warm will slow down their laying, or may stop all together.

- Provide plenty of shade in the run to allow the chickens escape from the sunshine.

- If possible keep hen house walls removable, and put mesh screens in to allow increased air circulation.

- Fermentation increases in hot weather. Hen houses need to be cleaned out more frequently to prevent infestation and illness.

- Ensure plenty of fresh cool water is available at all time.

- Chickens tend to eat less in the heat. Offer them salad greens and seed to entice their appetites.

- Keep their dust bath refilled and add delousing and anti-mite powder to keep your chickens free from parasites.

# Introducing new birds

How to introduce new chickens is widely debated. The method of introduction really depends on the age of the chickens.

### New adult chickens

If the new chickens are of similar size to your existing flock then the introduction should be fairly easy. Place your new chickens into the chicken coop just after dark. All the chickens will be at their most relaxed. Sleeping in the chicken house will establish a home roost for the new chicken and they will return to it each evening. When the morning comes there will be the odd push and shove as they assess each other and establish the pecking order. This is very occasionally dramatic. To humans it can look very cruel to watch our beloved birds shun or peck at each other. Rest assured they will find a happy balance. If at any time a chicken begins to bleed remove them from the flock immediately. Chickens cannot help themselves from pecking at a wound, and this will quickly develop into a large open sore. To reduce their feelings of competitiveness sprinkle feed over a wide area to reduce their need to jostle at a feeder. If you are introducing an ex-bat hen, do ensure they have no wounds and are feeling bright and energetic.

'Provide plenty of shade in the run to allow the chickens escape from the sunshine.'

## Introducing younger birds

If you have hatched your own chicks, or have purchased some younger pullets it can be a little tricky to integrate them into the flock. They are not big enough to stand their ground to a larger chicken and will be bullied out of the feed.

If there is space in your hen house place a large dog crate inside. Keep your younger hens inside the dog crate for a few days and allow the chickens to become used to the sight and smell of each other. When you release the young chickens they will stand a far better chance of automatic acceptance.

If your hen house is not large enough, you could place the younger birds in an enclosed run alongside the older chickens' run, or in a small run within the chickens' run. Again they will be able to familiarise themselves and be less prone to quarrel.

'Place your new chickens into the chicken coop just after dark.'

# Summing Up

- Free range is a term that is often used loosely. The most important factor to keep in mind is that all chickens deserve the space to behave like a normal chicken.

- If you have sprightly chickens and a low fence then it may be best to clip their wings. Trim only the flight feathers and be careful of the feather shafts.

- The deep litter method is a low maintenance method of chicken coop care. This method can add extra insulation through the coldest part of the year.

- Chickens thrive on predictability. Let them out and feed them on a schedule and they will be a happy flock.

- Winter months can freeze drinkers and even eggs. Check on your chickens regularly to keep them hydrated and to limit mess.

- Chickens are not known for their welcoming sense of community. They may need time to familiarise themselves and work out their pecking order.

# Chapter Eight

# Hatching and Brooding

## Broody hen

A broody hen is a chicken that has decided she must produce chicks. A hen will go through a broody cycle depending on her environment, breed and individual temperament. Some chickens are keen mothers, while others will never express an interest. It is very difficult to slow a hen's determination to produce chicks once she has made up her mind. A hen can be extraordinarily stubborn and she will sit and brood on anything from an egg to a golf ball. You will notice a difference in her appearance as she spreads herself out width ways and appears to have almost doubled in size. Hens are more likely to go broody in the spring, and in their second year of life, however they can and will do so at any time or age that suits them. Many breeds of chicken have been bred to reduce broody behaviour as a broody hen will stop laying. Commercial varieties will rarely go broody, whereas, Silkies and Pekins are known for their mothering skills.

A hen will sit on eggs for weeks on end. Despite eggs taking only 21 days to hatch, a hen will sit as long as it takes. If you do not have a cockerel, you might consider getting your hen some fertile eggs to hatch rather than have her waste her time sitting with no results. Hens will forgo their own needs and unless watched carefully their health may deteriorate. If you wish for your hen to hatch her eggs it is prudent to provide her a separate pen from the rest of her flock if at all possible. The chicks that hatch may come to harm under the scrutiny of the other flock members.

'Many breeds of chicken have been bred to reduce broody behaviour as a broody hen will stop laying.'

# Fertile cockerel

In order to produce fertile eggs, you will need a fertile cockerel. Cockerels have been known to begin mounting hens from as early as ten weeks. At this young age they tend to have a lower sperm count and will not consistently fertilise the hens. Most breeders prefer to use cockerels of around a year old for breeding purposes as they are at their fertile peak. However, their fertility is regulated by the length of daylight, nutrition, bodyweight and testosterone levels. As a cockerel ages he will lose fertility, and after the age of five can no longer be relied upon for producing fertile eggs. It is important to choose a cockerel of similar size to your hens to achieve the best fertility rate and to avoid injuring a hen. Do not pair up a large fowl cockerel with bantams.

# Are my eggs fertile?

If you break an egg open into a dish and look closely at the yolk you should be able to identify a small white mark. If this mark is perfectly round and the centre is yellow, than your egg is fertile. This is called a blastoderm as the cell has divided and fertalisation has taken place. If the mark is completely white and uneven, than your egg is infertile, and the mark is called a blastodisc.

# Using an incubator

Every brand of incubator will come with a manual that is specific to the model you have purchased. This will contain the necessary instructions to set the incubator how you want it.

There are several steps that you can take to maximise your egg's chance of becoming a chick.

### Getting ready for incubation

- Set the incubator up in a place that the temperature will not vary. Window ledges, bathrooms and kitchens tend to fluctuate their humidity and temperature frequently.

'If you break an egg open into a dish and look closely at the yolk you should be able to identify a small white mark. If this mark is perfectly round and the centre is yellow, than your egg is fertile.'

- Do not set your incubator up in the bedroom you sleep in. This can cause an allergic reaction in some people.

- Calibrate the incubator and allow it to run for 24 hours before setting the eggs.

- Store your eggs pointed end down, between 40°F/ 4.5°C and 70°F/ 21.1°C for up to seven days.

The temperature to incubate chicken eggs is between 37.4°C and 37.6°C. The humidity needs to measure an average of 50-65% for the first 18 days. For the last three days and through hatching the humidity must be raised to 80%. This will ensure the chicks do not become stuck in the membrane. It can be quite an apprehensive experience watching your chicks hatch for the first time. A chick can take several hours from first pip to a full hatch. Resist the temptation to open the incubator and assist the chicks in hatching. Healthy chicks will hatch on their own and need the humidity and temperature to remain constant. Keep the incubator's air vent open through out the hatch to ensure air circulation.

## Setting your eggs

- Allow your eggs to come up to room temperature before placing in the incubator to prevent sweating.

- Keep the large end of the egg up.

- The temperature in the incubator will drop when the eggs are first set. This is okay. Let the incubator come back up to temperature. If you increase the temperature too quickly it will kill the embryos.

- If your incubator does not have an automatic turning cradle you will need to turn your eggs manually. Rotate the eggs 180 degrees, keeping the wide end up, at least three times a day. Turn the eggs an odd number of times each day to ensure the egg rests on the opposite side at night.

- For chicken eggs, stop turning the eggs on day 18 and increase the humidity.

Different species of birds have different incubation and humidity needs. Duck eggs take 28 days to hatch and require a high humidity.

# Candling

Candling your eggs is an exciting and easy way to check your eggs for fertility. Once your eggs have been set in the incubator for seven days you can take them out, and using a candling torch, shine a light through them. Candling allows you to check for eggs which are not developing, and you can then discard these. Leaving bad eggs in the incubator can lead to the unpleasant experience of having an egg explode or ooze in the incubator. This may contaminate the other eggs, and will cause a horrible smell.

On day seven you should be able to see a spider web of veins and an embryo sitting to one side. In light shelled eggs you can sometimes see the tiny heart beating.

By day fourteen, two thirds of the egg will appear dark as the developing chick has grown very rapidly. It will be difficult to see fine details, but movements will be visible.

'Candling your eggs is an exciting and easy way to check your eggs for fertility.'

Checking throughout your incubation will allow you to identify potential problems. An embryo that stops developing can be due to a number of factors. Incubation technique, storage of eggs prior to incubating, or infection from bacteria, can all lead to embryos failing to thrive.

If a red ring is seen inside the egg this is a sign of bacterial infection. Ensure your incubator is thoroughly disinfected before setting another batch of eggs.

## Candling troubleshooting

**Some of my eggs are candling clear on day seven. Are they infertile?**

It may be that the clear eggs were genuinely infertile. It is not unusual. However, it is likely that the eggs were stored at an incorrect temperature or in an incorrect position prior to incubation.

**Why did my embryos stop growing?**

Embryos may fail to thrive if the temperature fluctuates or if they have insufficient ventilation. It is also important to ensure the eggs are carefully turned at regular intervals.

**My chicks pipped but then died?**

This is a sad case, and is mostly likely due to poor nutrition in the breeding hens or due to disease.

**Why are my chicks hatching on day 19? Are they meant to be so noisy?**

Early chicks have been incubated at too high a temperature. Check that your thermometer is correct. They will be very noisy as they are premature and take a little while to adjust.

**It is day 22 and my eggs have started to pip. Will my chicks be okay?**

Chicks that are born late tend to be soft and lethargic. This may be due to old eggs being used or the temperature being too low in the incubator. The chicks will need extra care to ensure they start eating and drinking.

# Caring for chicks

Newly hatched chicks are both adorable and hard work in equal measure. They will need to be checked on every couple of hours each day for the first four weeks of life. If you work away from home it may be best to plan your chicks to your holiday schedule as chicks really do need someone around at all times.

Once you have decided you are going to rear chicks, the next issue is where to house them. A draught-proof room in your home or garage is ideal. Chicks create a lot of dust as they scratch about in their bedding. This can make quite a lot of mess. They also produce an odour that may not be suited to all noses. If you have cats, dogs or small children, it will be important to consider how best to prevent the chicks from harm's way.

# Brooder

Brooders of all shapes and sizes are available from pet and farm shops. They are easily manufactured at home and, unless you would like to spend the money on a packaged version, quite cheap to set up. The primary need for the

'Newly hatched chicks are both adorable and hard work in equal measure.'

chicks, apart from food and water, is heat. Newly hatched chicks are wet and need a lot of heat to dry and fluff up. They then need to be kept warm and fluffy, despite their endless attempts to bath in their drinking water.

The first week chicks need their air temperature to be up around 95 degrees, the second week it can be reduced to 90 degrees. Each week you will need to reduce the temperature by about 5 degrees until they are ready to transition to the outdoors.

The cheapest and easiest way to achieve this is to hang a heat lamp. A heat lamp can be anything from a 60 watt bulb for a small hatch of 2 chicks, to a 250 watt bulb for up 20 chicks. It is almost always better to have several and larger heat lamps instead of just one. The chicks may pile on top of one another to be close to the lamp and this will suffocate the ones on the bottom.

By having more than one lamp you can choose to turn on one or more in different combinations to adjust the heat to achieve the desired temperature. By raising the heat lamp you will also begin to lower the temperature. Heat lamps come in red and white light. Red light is generally preferred as white light is hard on the chicks' eyes and is difficult to fall asleep under. Red light will also prevent chicks from pecking at each other.

'If you have hens that are beautiful examples of their breed, and are productive layers then you may choose to breed them for replacement.'

This may sound very complicated. You do not need to worry about temperature being a difficult matter. Keep no more than eight chicks to a heat lamp and ensure they are out of any draught. If the chicks are cheeping in a low and regular way they are happy. Happy chicks will spread out and lounge around beneath the heat lamp. The time to worry is if your chicks begin cheeping in a high pitch and are huddling together. They are too cold. It is very important to keep chicks warm or they will give up on life.

## Bedding

Chicks eat and drink a lot as they are growing rapidly. Pine shavings or frequently changed paper towel is an excellent bedding choice as it is very absorbent. Do not use pine shavings immediately after hatch. The shavings will stick to the wet chick and the chicks will eat the shavings as they look for food. Lay a layer of quilted kitchen towel over the pine shavings for the first few days and change this every two hours. The bedding you choose must not be too smooth or slick. Chicks' legs are not very strong and they will easily developed splayed legs.

# Breeding for replacement

If you have hens that are beautiful examples of their breed, and are productive layers then you may choose to breed them for replacement. Ageing happens to all of us, chickens included. A hen that lays well in her first year will decline in the next, and again in the following year. If you are concerned about egg production then this may lead you to consider breeding your flock.

The first season of breeding is relatively straightforward. As long as your hens and cockerel are not related then they can breed as they wish. The difficulty comes in breeding sustainably over many generations. The viability of future generations is reliant on careful breeding without genetic degradation.

## Which chickens should I breed?

- Breeding your best hen to your best cockerel is called improvement breeding. This will be successful in producing an improved flock for the next generation.

- To conserve the genetic diversity in your flock, separate your hens into three groups, and use leg rings to mark them. Breeding each group of hens to different cockerels will allow you to keep the maximum amount of variation.

- If you only keep one cockerel, he is half your flock by genes. It may be best to swap cockerels with another breeder to keep the relationships between the chickens as varied as possible.

Done well, breeding for replacement keeps and improves breed standards and supports chicken breeders the world over.

'Done well, breeding for replacement keeps and improves breed standards and supports chicken breeders the world over.'

# Preventing broodiness

There are many suggestions to prevent broodiness, from dunking a hen in cold water to simply removing the eggs and leaving her with nothing to sit on. Neither of these are good solutions. A wet chicken will very quickly become a sick chicken. A hen that has a penchant for raising some chicks will beg, borrow and steal some eggs if she loses her own.

The best way to discourage broodiness is to change the environment the hen prefers to be broody in. A broody hen will seek a warm, dark and draught-free place to nest. If you can change this she will soon change her mind and her broodiness will pass. It may be that shutting her out of the coop during the day, provided the weather is good, is enough. Putting a battery-operated lantern in her preferred nest box and removing the bedding can be effective. Sometimes being a chicken keeper means finding a creative solution that will work for you and your flock. A football blocking the nest box may be the solution that works most effectively for your hen.

'The best way to discourage broodiness is to change the environment the hen prefers to be broody in.'

# Summing Up

- A broody hen is a determined mum-to-be. She will be protective and refuse to leave her nest.

- Cocks need to be a similar size to the hens. A large fowl cock could injure or kill a bantam.

- Read your incubator's manual and set it up well ahead of setting your eggs.

- Keep your eggs large end up in a cool place ahead of incubating.

- During the last three days of incubation the humidity must be raised to ensure a safe hatch.

- Do not open the incubator to check and assist chicks in hatching. This disrupts both the temperature and the humidity.

- Chicken eggs will take on average 21 days to hatch.

- Eggs can be candled to check for fertility from day seven onwards.

- A brooder will keep your chicks warm and dry after they hatch.

- Breeding is not as easy as it sounds and careful consideration needs to be given to the maintenance of your flock's genetic diversity.

- There are a number of recommended solutions to help prevent broodiness. The most effective being to change the environment the hen prefers to be broody in.

# Chapter Nine

# Eggs and More Eggs

## Collecting eggs

To get the best from your eggs you need to know how to properly handle them. The quality of your eggs is dependent upon how you manage your chickens and the conditions in which you keep your eggs.

## What can I do?

- Keep the chickens' nest boxes clean and dry. Dirty eggs lead to contamination.

- Ensure there is a minimum of one nest box to every four hens. This will limit egg breakage and reduce soiled nests.

- Collect eggs promptly. Most hens will have laid by mid-morning, and the longer an egg stays in the nest the longer its risk of losing condition.

- Place newly collected eggs in an easy to clean container. Do not use a metal basket as this may rust. The rust can stain and soil the eggs.

- Wash eggs before cooling them. When washing eggs use water ten degrees warmer than the egg. The warm water will prevent the pores of the egg from contracting and pulling the dirt into the egg. Do not leave eggs to sit in water. Once the eggs have become the same temperature as the water they can take in bacteria from the water.

- Dry and then chill the eggs immediately after washing them.

'The quality of your eggs is dependent upon how you manage your chickens and the conditions in which you keep your eggs.'

# Storing eggs

※ Eggs should be placed large end up in an egg carton to keep their air cell stable.

※ Keep the temperature of the eggs between 50-55°F and a 70-70% humidity.

※ Store eggs separate from other items that produce an odour. Onions, fish and potatoes will cause the eggs to develop an unpleasant flavour.

※ Date the egg carton to avoid confusion between older and newer eggs. Try to consume all eggs before they are three weeks old.

※ Do not leave eggs at room temperature or in warm conditions. Eggs decline rapidly in warm, dry environments.

※ If an egg has a weak or unusually shaped shell discard the egg or consume promptly. A thin shell may go off more quickly.

# Bad egg test

An egg that has spoiled will release a very unpleasant smell if broken open. Should you be unsure if an egg is safe to eat there is a simple way to check without risking a disagreeable surprise:

※ Fill a deep bowl with at least 6 inches of water.

※ Gently lower the egg into the water.

※ Observe the egg.

A fresh egg will stay on the bottom of the bowl. It will remain on its side as the air cell in the egg is relatively small. The egg will feel substantially heavy.

An older egg will have had more air enter it. As the amount of air inside the shell increases, the egg will stand upright and begin to float. The small end of the egg will stay pointed down, and the larger end will point towards the surface of the water. If the egg simply stands up but is still touching the bottom of the bowl it is still safe to eat.

Eggs that float in the water and do not touch the bottom of the bowl are quite possibly bad and are certainly old. They should be discarded.

Bad eggs tend to feel quite light in comparison to a fresh egg. If you would prefer to crack the egg open, you can tell an egg's age by evaluating the yolk and the white.

Break the egg open onto a flat plate.

A fresh egg will have a round neat yolk that sits surrounded by thick egg white. The egg white is cloudy immediately after being laid as it contains carbon dioxide which slowly dissipates.

As eggs age their yolk becomes flatter and the white becomes thinner.

# Freezing and preserving eggs

Should you be in the fortunate position to have a surplus of eggs, there are a number of ways to preserve and use them.

## Freezing eggs

Eggs can be frozen and kept for up to six months. To freeze an egg it must be removed from its shell. Then you can decide if you would prefer to freeze the whole egg, or to separate the white and the yolk prior to freezing. It is useful to freeze eggs in quantities that you will use regularly. Ice cube trays are handy for freezing single egg whites or yolks. Ensure that all eggs are labelled with both the date and quantity. Egg yolks will change texture during the freezing and thawing process. To avoid the yolk becoming too thick add a pinch of salt to the yolk if it is destined to be used in a savory recipe. If the yolk is needed for a sweet recipe, add a pinch of sugar.

## Pickled eggs

Served in a salad or alongside a ploughman's lunch, pickled eggs are delicious. Choose only the freshest and best of your eggs. Boil them until hard in the centre. The freshest produce will always preserve the best, and keep the maximum amount of their nutrition. Once the eggs have boiled sufficiently, cool them immediately in a large basin of cold water. Peel away the shell. This may be quite difficult with freshly laid eggs as the egg white has a tendency to stick

'Bad eggs tend to feel quite light in comparison to a fresh egg. A fresh egg will have a round neat yolk that sits surrounded by thick egg white.'

to the inner shell membrane. Place the peeled eggs in a sterile pickling jar until the jar is filled. Bring the pickling vinegar and spices to a boil and simmer for ten minutes. Pour it into the jar until the eggs are completely covered. Seal the jar and store in the fridge for 3-4 months.

## British pub pickled eggs

6 hard boiled eggs

2 cups of malt vinegar

1 finely chopped chilli pepper

6 black peppercorns

6 whole cloves

1 cinnamon stick

½ tsp of all spice

½ tsp mixed spice

## Dilled eggs

6 hard boiled eggs

1½ cups of white vinegar

1 cup dill weed

¼ tsp white pepper

3 tsp salt

¼ tsp mustard seed

½ tsp finely chopped onion

½ tsp minced garlic

# Omelettes to face masks

## Cooking eggs

Fresh eggs will produce the most amazing poached and fried eggs. Older eggs will do a fine job in cakes, omelettes, or as a home-made beauty treatment.

### Boiling an egg

Boiled eggs can range from a perfectly cooked soft boiled egg to a rubber ball. For a soft boiled egg, place the egg in a pan of salted boiling water. The egg will be ready in thee and a half minutes for a very small egg to six minutes for a very large egg. For a hard boiled egg, leave the egg to boil for a full ten minutes. Placing an egg in a pan of cold water and cooking for up to twenty minutes will produce a very tough egg. Salting the water helps to ease peeling the shells afterwards. Adding a teaspoon of vinegar to the water will help prevent any egg whites from running out should the eggs crack.

### Poaching eggs

A poached egg is a simple delight and a great way to showcase a fresh egg. Fill a pan with water and bring it to a gentle simmer. Crack an egg into a cup and gently slide the egg into the water. Cook the egg for between two and four minutes to achieve your preferred texture.

### Scrambled eggs

Scrambled eggs are an easy childhood favourite. Whisk the eggs together with a tablespoon of milk per egg. Season with salt and pepper and stir in a little wholegrain mustard if so desired. Melt a knob of butter in a pan and add the eggs. Stir constantly over medium heat until the mixture is set.

'A poached egg is a simple delight and a great way to showcase a fresh egg.'

## Omelettes

Whisk a tablespoon of water with two or three eggs and season with salt and pepper. Melt a knob of butter in a pan and pour the eggs in. Scatter your choice of toppings onto the eggs, and run a spatula around the edge of the pan to keep the eggs from sticking. Once the eggs has set, fold it in half and serve. Alternately, use an oven proof pan and place the eggs under the grill for 8-12 minutes.

## Quiche

Whisk three eggs and one cup of double cream together. Add your favourite quiche ingredients. For Quiche Lorraine, add 200g chopped, cooked, streaky bacon, 80g of grated cheddar and a pinch of nutmeg. Pour over a blind baked pastry crust and place in a preheated oven at 150°C for 35 minutes.

## Meringues

Beat two egg whites in a clean mixing bowl until white and stands in stiff peaks. Add 55g of icing sugar and 55g of caster sugar slowly, one spoonful at a time, and continue mixing. When the mixture is smooth and fluffy, spoon onto a lined baking sheet in nests. Place in a pre-heated oven at 100°C for 1½ hours. Turn the oven off and leave the meringues to cool inside the oven.

## Custard

Using the two yolks left over from the meringues you can now make a delicious custard. Add 50g of caster sugar to the yolks and whisk until pale. Next, whisk in a half teaspoon of cornflour.

Place a teaspoon of vanilla bean paste, 150ml of full fat milk and 150ml of single cream in a pan and gently bring it almost to boiling. Slowly pour the milk mixture over the egg yolks and whisk.

Return the mixture to the pan and stir continuously over a low heat until it thickens. This should take around five minutes.

# Beauty products

With chickens in the garden you really do not need to spend money on expensive beauty products. Eggs will make a wonderful treatment for many hair and skin problems.

## Hair

To improve oily hair whisk an egg white and massage outward from your scalp. Leave the egg white in for 20 minutes and then shampoo as normal.

For dry hair, use a teaspoon of olive oil whisked into a single egg yolk. Work the egg mixture into the hair and leave in for 20 minutes. To rinse it out shampoo your hair as normal.

To add body and shine to your hair, beat a whole egg with the juice of a lemon. Apply the mixture to your hair and leave in for up to 30 minutes. Shampoo as usual to rinse the mixture out.

It is important not to use very hot water when rinsing egg out of your hair as you do not want to cook the egg!

'Eggs will make a wonderful treatment for many hair and skin problems.'

## Skin

**Face mask to tighten the skin**

Whip an egg white until foamy. Spread the egg white evenly onto your face and let it dry. Wash the dried egg away with cool water and your skin will feel tighter and evenly toned.

**Face mask for blemishes**

Whisk an egg with a teaspoon of honey. Apply it evenly to your face and allow to set for 20 minutes. Rinse with cool water.

### Exfoliating and toning face scrub

Mix an egg with a teaspoon of rolled oats, and a half teaspoon of lemon juice. Gently scrub the mixture onto the skin and rinse with cool water.

Stir in a teaspoon of honey and a teaspoon of olive oil.

## Foot rubs

### For dry and sore feet

Squeeze a capsule of evening primrose oil into a bowl with an egg yolk and one teaspoon fine seasalt. Mix well and then gently massage into your feet. Leave for 20 minutes before washing off with warm water.

### For callused heels

Soak one egg yolk in a half cup of rice wine for three days. Blend the yolk and the rice wine before applying to the heels. Leave the yolk on for one hour before washing off.

# Summing Up

- Keep your nest boxes clean, dark and quiet.

- Eggs should be kept cool and stored on their point.

- You can test an egg to see how much air has entered the porous shell. This will help determine how fresh it is.

- Only freeze eggs after they have been removed from their shell.

- Eggs have been used for centuries in hair and skin products. There are many recipes for you to try.

# Chapter Ten

# Animal Welfare: Five Freedoms

The Five Freedoms were developed by the Farm Animal Welfare Council (FAWC). The Five Freedoms create a framework of ideals to ensure all animals have the highest standard of care. This may sound very complicated. Do not be wary of these standards. They are basic ideals of compassion and empathy which anyone with a pet would employ without a second thought.

**The Five Freedoms are best employed when:**

- The environment has been suitably adapted for the animals.
- The animal caregivers have the knowledge and skills relevant to their animals.
- Conscious and responsible planning ahead of acquiring the animals.
- Transport is conducted as gently as possible.
- When necessary, animals are dispatched humanely.

'The Five Freedoms create a framework of ideals to ensure all animals have the highest standard of care.'

## 1 – Freedom from hunger or thirst

Chickens have a right to access fresh water at all times. They are entitled to a suitable diet which maintains and promotes their health. The Food and Agriculture Organization held a meeting to discuss how the correct food and adequate water reduces stress and suffering for all animals. Before acquiring chickens read chapter 3 to ensure you have a good understanding of a chicken's diet. Once you are aware of what your chicken needs, it is easy to protect them from unnecessary physical and psychological suffering.

## 2 – Freedom from discomfort

Chicken keepers have a duty to provide a safe and comfortable environment. This environment needs to be suitable to the normal habits and needs of chickens. Chickens need protection from the elements and predators. Chapter 4 considers various factors in choosing the correct housing and creating a safe environment for your birds.

## 3 – Freedom from pain, injury or disease

While no one can keep their animals safe from ever becoming ill, it is important that basic preventative steps are taken. Basic hygiene and routine care is the key to prevention. Should one of your chickens become ill you need to seek appropriate treatment quickly and not allow the bird to suffer. Chapter 6 provides information on common ailments, and the help list is a good reference for finding an experienced person for assistance should your chickens require special care.

'Chicken keepers have a duty to ensure that none of their chickens are treated or kept in such a way which could cause mental anguish or suffering.'

## 4 – Freedom to express normal behaviour

A chicken should have access to sufficient and suitable space for it to behave like a normal chicken. They have the right to have the facilities to perform their instinctive behaviours. Chickens are not lone animals and require the company of other chickens. Just as you would not keep a cat in an aquarium, chickens have unique needs. Chapter 7 looks at many of the ways chickens express themselves and what you can do to best accommodate them.

## 5 – Freedom from fear or distress

Chicken keepers have a duty to ensure that none of their chickens are treated or kept in such a way which could cause mental anguish or suffering. This is primarily focused towards chickens being raised for meat. However, this will be an issue for all chicken keepers during transit, or when there is environmental changes. In the changing seasons chickens will require different levels of care. Chickens progress through several life stages which have specific needs.

# Welfare codes

The Department for Environment, Food & Rural Affairs (Defra) maintains a database of codes of recommendations for the welfare of livestock. Each animal has a specific welfare code to outline the recommended high standards of animal care for all livestock.

While the codes are not statutory requirements, all farm workers and animal keepers are required by law to be familiar with the relevant codes.

There are specific standards outlined by the RSPCA for all aspects of a chicken's life.

## Chicks

The standard of care for chicks is outlined based on age:

- Day-old chicks need to be handled as little and as carefully as possible.

- Chickens need to be exposed to natural daylight before their seventh day.

- At all times, the chick's environmental temperature must be monitored. Stress due to heat or cold is a serious concern.

- Chicks need to be checked on frequently.

- Feeders and drinkers need to be kept clean. This is more difficult than it might sound, especially as chicks become older.

- Chicks should not be moved from one building to another more than once during their brooding period. Chicks do not handle extreme changes well. Therefore, they need the first six to eight weeks of their life to be quite consistent.

- Any changes in diet should be made gradually over a three-day period.

- Chickens should be introduced to their outdoor run by 28 days old.

## Older chickens

- Feed should be made readily available and at more than one location to prevent bullying.

- There must be litter covering the whole of the chicken house floor.

- Requirements state that at least 8 hours of daylight and a minimum of 6 hours of complete darkness are necessary each day.

- Chickens must be humanely killed without delay if they are in severe and uncontrollable pain or are so severely disabled they cannot eat, drink or walk.

- Chickens must have access to appropriate shelter.

## Managing your chickens

'If any of your birds become sick or are in distress you have a duty to provide immediate care and attention.'

The primary task that will ensure good chicken management is to be aware of what is normal chicken behaviour and what is a sign of illness. By taking the time to watch your chickens each day, you will be able to quickly identify any sick or injured birds. If any of your birds become sick or are in distress you have a duty to provide immediate care and attention. If you are unable to solve the problem a veterinarian should be consulted as soon as possible.

**Signs of healthy chickens:**

- The chickens should have clear and bright eyes.

- Their posture should be upright and normal for their breed.

- The chickens should be energetic and inquisitive.

- Feeding and drinking should be in-keeping with the flock's normal appetite. This will vary depending on the weather and time of day.

- Feathers and skin should be clean and healthy in appearance.

**Signs of poor or declining health:**

- A reduced appetite or thirst despite access to food and water.

- A chicken which preens excessively.

- Chickens may talk constantly and in an unusual tone.

- Hyperactivity can be a sign of nervousness or discomfort.

- A reduction in egg production or egg quality, such as shell defects, may be due to health-related issues.

# Registering a flock

Anyone raising chickens is encouraged to voluntarily notify Defra. Many chicken keepers only have a few chickens in their garden, and as such they are not required to register their flock with Defra. Should it increase in size, you are required to register your flock once you have 50 birds. It is worth noting that this total applies to all poultry. If you have 20 ducks, 20 chickens and 10 turkeys, you have a duty to register.

## Why is registering so important?

- To help keep the national records as accurate as possible.

- It allows Defra to easily contact you in the event of a potential disease outbreak.

- When disease prevention and treatments are being allocated, poultry that is not registered may not receive the resources they need.

'Should your flock increase in size, you are required to register your flock once you have 50 birds.'

# Summing Up

- There is no need to feel overwhelmed by animal welfare regulations.

- Take the time to plan how and where you want to house your chickens.

- If there is anything you are unsure about, then ask questions. The RSPCA and Defra are there to assist people in caring for their animals. See the help list for their contact details.

- Enjoy your chickens. If you are happy, the chances are good that your chickens are content.

- Confidence comes with time. As you get to know your individual flock you will find the best way that works for you.

# Glossary

**Aspergillosis**
An umbrella name given to a variety of infections which are caused by the inhalation of fungal mould.

**Bantam**
Describes a small chicken with no large breed equivalent. Many small breed chickens may be described as bantams but are in fact simply a miniature version of a bigger chicken.

**Broody**
When a hen develops the unstoppable inclination to sit and hatch eggs.

**Candle**
The inspection of an egg's contents by shining a strong light through the shell.

**Cock**
A male chicken that has had his first moult.

**Cockerel**
A male chicken before his first moult.

**Cecum**
A small pouch at the end of the juncture between the small and large intestines. Often called the chicken appendix.

**Cloaca**
The space just inside the vent where the chicken's urinary, digestive and reproductive tract all meet up.

**Comb**
The prominent red fleshy piece atop a chicken's head.

**Coop**
The name given to a chicken's home.

**Cuticle**
The disease-resistant barrier that is put on the egg in the final stages of production within the hen.

**Drinker**
A water container for chickens.

**Dust bath**
A dusty or sandy area in which chickens bath to remove mites and lice from their feathers.

**Flight feathers**
When the wing is outstretched the flight feathers are the very largest feathers at the edge.

**Grit**
Small stones that are used by chickens to break down their food.

**Hen**
A female chicken that has completed her first period of laying.

**Hybrids**
Chickens that have been bred from two breeds to combine the best characteristics from both.

**Incubation**
To provide the ideal conditions for a chicken egg to hatch over a period of 21 days.

**Keel**
The chicken's breastbone.

**Moult**
A six to eight week annual period where the chicken sheds and replaces its feathers.

**Nematode**
A parasitic roundworm, which is frequently found in poultry.

**Oocyst**
Fertilised eggs from highly infectious parasites.

**Oviduct**
The reproductive tract of the chicken which the egg passes through.

**Pellet**
Feed that has been mashed and then pressed together into small pieces.

### Point of lay

Once a pullet has reached 18 weeks she may be called point of lay, though it may be another four weeks before she lays her first egg.

### Pullet

A young female chicken that has not yet completed her first laying season.

### Scales

The skin that covers the legs and toes.

### Vent

The exit point for all digestive matter and eggs.

### Wattles

The flaps of flesh that hang down from beneath either side of the chicken's beak.

# Help List

## Helplines

### Environmental Agency Helpline

Tel: 03708 506 506

### RSPCA Helpline/Cruelty line

Tel: 0300 1234 999

### VMD Helpline

Tel: 01932 336 911
The Veterinary Medicine Department offers guidance on everything from illness to appropriate record keeping for administering medications.


## Online Forums/Websites and Clubs

### Bird Trader

www.birdtrader.co.uk
Friday Media Group
London Rd
Sayers Common
East Sussex
BN6 9HS
Email: info@birdtrader.co.uk
Tel: 01646 680 733
A useful site for finding chickens for sale in your area. The site also features a forum and useful articles on health and welfare.

## Dragonflies and Dandelions

www.dlhunicorn.conforums.comi
A very useful international forum. If you ever have a question or concern this site will have plenty of information from other chicken keepers to help you solve your problem.

## Hen Rehoming Hub

www.exbatteryhens.org.uk
This site is useful for anyone considering rehoming ex-battery hens. There is a useful search engine to assist you in finding your area. They have the contact details for all the rehoming organisations throughout the United Kingdom

## Poultry Club

www.poultryclub.org
The Poultry Club of Great Britain offers useful advice from proper care to breed lists. They maintain contact details for breed clubs and societies.

## The Poultry Pages

www.poultry.allotment.org.uk
This website has a great section on poultry. From their comprehensive charts on egg colours to finding a poultry keeping course in your area, there is a wealth of information for all chicken keepers.

## The Poultry Site

www.thepoultrysite.com
Dedicated to providing information on every aspect of caring for poultry. This site has an excellent Quick Disease Guide.

## The Rare Breeds Survival Trust

www.rbst.org.uk
Stoneleigh Park
Nr Kenilworth
Warwickshire
CV8 2LG
Tel: 024 7669 6551
Email: enquiries@rbst.org.uk

A charity which was founded to protect all native breeds of farm animals. They offer assistance and support to those searching for rare breed livestock. The trust provides advice on starting with rare breeds and on breeding programmes. They aim to promote knowledge and to conserve the United Kingdom's rare breeds.

## Rare Poultry Society

www.rarepoultrysociety.co.uk
The rare poultry society began with the intent to provide care for rare and endangered breeds which do not have a breed specific club or society.

# Professional Organisations

## Animal Health Alerts

www.animalhealth.defra.gov.uk/alerts
Tel: 0844 88 44 600
This website allows you to sign up to be alerted to the most up-to-date information on animal disease. It also includes a comprehensive veterinarian search facility.

## British Free Range Egg Producers Association (BFREPA)

www.theranger.co.uk
PO Box 3425
Ashton Keynes
Swindon
SN6 6WR
Tel: 01285 869 913
This association publishes a magazine for the free-range egg section and supports and promotes the benefits of free-range farming. They negotiate on behalf of free-range farmers and support their members through an experienced support system and a huge data bank. The website has all the up-to-date information a chicken keeper could ask for, from flock health and feed prices to the latest industry news.

## Department for Environment, Food & Rural Affairs (Defra)

www.defra.gov.uk
Nobel House
17 Smith Square
London
SW1P 3JR
Tel: 08459 335 577
The Department for Environment, Food & Rural Affairs is a huge organisation that can offer advice and assistance on all aspects of marketing rules and regulations. They provide regular updates regarding welfare standards and disease outbreaks.

## Great Britain Poultry Register

http://poultry.defra.gov.uk
Tel: 0800 634 1112
Established by Defra, to gather and record essential information about certain species of birds kept in the UK.

## National Office of Animal Health (NOAH)

www.noahcompendium.co.uk
3 Crossfield Chambers
Gladbeck Way
Enfield
EN2 7HF
Tel: 020 8367 3131
Email: noah@noah.co.uk
NOAH is the UK animal medicine industry's representative figure. NOAH acts as both a consultative and communication organisation for animal medications and health.

## RSPCA

www.rspca.org.uk
The RSPCA works to educate pet owners and to protect animals from mistreatment. They have detailed booklets regarding the care and welfare of chickens which have been developed by poultry welfare specialists. These booklets are free to read online.

# Book List

**Impact Of Animal Nutrition On Animal Welfare 2012**
Food and Agriculture Organization. (Available from http://www.fao.org/)

**Poultry Farming: Welfare Regulations 2012**
Department for Environment & Rural Affairs. (Available from https://www.gov.uk/poultry-welfare-guidance-on-the-farm)

**Protect Your Birds From the Risk of Disease 2012**
Department for Environment & Rural Affairs. (Available from http://www.defra.gov.uk/)

**Welfare Standards for Chickens 2011**
RSPCA. (Available from http://www.rspca.org.uk/sciencegroup/farmanimals/standards/chickens)

# References

ADSA [Online] Available at: http://www.adas.co.uk/ [accessed on 28 October 2012]

British Hen Welfare Trust [Online] Available at: http://www.bhwt.org.uk [accessed on 28 October 2012]

Department of Health [Online] Available at: http://www.dh.gov.uk [accessed on 13 October 2012]

Omlet [Online] Available at: http://www.omlet.co.uk/breeds/chickens/ [accessed on 13 October 2012]

NFU [Online] Available at http://www.nfuonline.com/ [accessed on 22 October 2012]

Soil Association [Online] Available at: http://www.soilassociation.org [accessed on 8 October 2012]

The Accidental Smallholder [Online] Available at: http://www.accidentalsmallholder.net [accessed on 13 October 2012]

The Poultry Club Of Great Britain [Online] Available at: http://www.poultryclub.org/ [accessed on 8 October 2012]

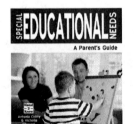  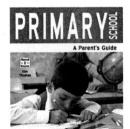  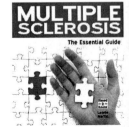